Educated Girl, Empowered Woman

The Art of Living with Grace, Joy, & Dignity

DR. SOLANGES VIVENS

EDUCATED GIRL, EMPOWERED WOMAN:
THE ART OF LIVING WITH GRACE, JOY, & DIGNITY

Copyright © 2023 Dr. Solanges Vivens

Published by Vivens Media Group

Cover Design: Lynda Valbrun-McKenzie and Roberto Nunez
Cover Photo: Daniella Monestime
Layout Design: Roberto Nunez

For special orders, quantity sales, course adoptions, and corporate sales, please contact the publisher at:

Vivens Media Group
531 Coconut Palm Terrace
Plantation, FL 33324
info@vivensmedia.com

ISBN: 979-8-9898620-0-9

Printed in the United States of America

Table of Contents

The Power to Move Mountains

From the distant shores of Haiti to the buzzing hub of America, I've traveled through life on a journey that has been anything but ordinary. Like a turtle carrying its home on its back, I've learned to carry my experiences, heritage, and stories with me, providing a hard shell of endurance against the unpredictable waves of life. From my childhood in Haiti, the turtle has always been a significant creature to me, representing resilience and patience. It is this symbolism that I carried with me throughout my journey, and you will find the turtle as a recurring symbol throughout this book, as it embodies the life I've lived. Turtles are mindful, adaptable, and courageous. They remind us that however fast the world may spin, we should move at our own pace, armored by our wisdom and powered by determination. In many ways, this book is my turtle shell, a collection of my narratives, lessons, trials, and triumphs.

The past seventy-seven years of my life have been filled with struggles and victories, grief and joy, obstacles and breakthroughs. From navigating the unfamiliar terrains of America, a foreign land that I came to call home, battling the all-too-real glass ceilings of racial discrimination in my professional journey, to grappling with the overwhelming responsibilities of running a multimillion-dollar business—each experience has shaped me. Through it all, I have embraced every setback as a setup for a comeback, every challenge as an opportunity for growth, and every loss as a step closer to my personal and professional evolution.

Like the turtle that retreats into its shell during times of danger and uncertainty, I, too, have learned to safeguard my spirit, nurturing an inner strength that has allowed me to bounce back from adversity time and time again. As I share my journey with you, I hope you find your inner turtle, that determined part of you that will move mountains to create a path forward.

The power to endure, persist, and overcome is a testament to the human spirit, a spirit that I've seen reflected in the faces of those I've served throughout my career, from infants to older adults. The myriad of emotions and experiences I've encountered in my life and work have woven a tapestry of life lessons, each thread a confirmation of the strength and spirit of humanity. This book is my attempt to share that tapestry with you.

In the following chapters, you will discover the story of a badass girl who dared to dream, dared to be, and dared to move mountains. This book is more than just my story; it is a celebration of empowerment and determination, and a tribute to all the women who dare to dream and dare to be.

I've often been told that I am a woman who lives life in vivid color, savoring every experience, every emotion, and every moment. This book is my palette, with each chapter a different color that paints the picture of my life. Some chapters are filled with bright and cheerful hues representing joyful times, others are imbued with dark and stormy shades, reflecting periods of struggle and adversity. But each hue contributes to the masterpiece that is my life.

I invite you to journey with me, to laugh with me, to cry with me, to celebrate with me, and to discover with me. As you turn these pages, may you find inspiration in my story, courage in my struggles, and hope in my victories. Just as the turtle moves at its own pace, I encourage you to take this journey at your own rhythm, soaking in each experience, each lesson, and each story as it resonates with you.

And always remember, no matter the speed, direction, or hurdles in your journey, like the turtle, you too, have the power to move mountains.

Solanges Vivens

CHAPTER ONE

A Senior Moment

In May 2002, I officially became a senior. I spent the first day of my fifty-fifth birthday in the sterile, antiseptic environment of Sibley Memorial Hospital in Washington, D.C., sitting at my husband's bedside. He had been at this hospital for over five days, a stay that felt like an eternity. Despite the parade of white-coated experts, no doctors could diagnose the cause of his illness. He looked at me with an expression that tore at my heart. His grip on my hand was weak, and his usually vibrant eyes were clouded over. Unaware, he had no notion that it was my birthday. Once sparkling with life and vitality, his eyes were now opaque with confusion and exhaustion.

To minimize his sadness, I felt it was unnecessary to remind him that it was my birthday. At this very sullen and somber moment, my heart heavy with a sorrow that words could barely express, I realized I had to learn quickly to move past my silent pain and showered him with love. Watching my tall, dark, handsome, and loving husband slowly fade away on a hospital bed was not how I envisioned my grand entry into the fifty-five and over category as we are labeled by society. This was no celebration, no jubilation—just a sobering welcome to a reality I hadn't expected.

At his bedside, fixated on his face, I imagined reading a lovely birthday card just like the ones he had given me every year. The memories floated gently, like sea turtles gliding in the vast, azure ocean. His cards usually carried just the perfect message that you would think he wrote himself. His cards always expressed precisely what he wanted to tell me from his heart. Oh, how I missed them today! Their heartfelt words were now mere echoes in my memory. I had saved all his prior cards as treasures of our love story. They always ended with his favorite two words: "Love, Keith."

That evening, once I arrived home from the hospital, the familiar scent of our shared life now tinged with the stark reality of his absence, I went straight to the box of old cards. I started to read over and over until I was exhausted. I crawled to my bed with no dinner and no shower. I recall waking up only to find myself in the same outfit I wore the day before, tears still damp on my cheeks and his words still resonating.

Just nine months earlier, in August 2001, we had cruised the Mediterranean to celebrate his sixty-fifth birthday. He was strong, vibrant, and full of life. We danced every night to the music of an Antiguan Caribbean band on board the Cunard cruise ship and collapsed in each other's arms until dawn. The echo of the music, the rhythm of the dance, and the warmth of his embrace were all still so vivid in my memory.

For about thirty years, we spoiled each other. I accept those moments without any regrets. Yet sitting at the hospital, in the cold, sterile room that bore no resemblance to our warm, cozy home, I realized I had to be strong and handle the present moment confidently. Like a turtle carrying the weight of its shell, I bore the weight of my circumstances with bravery and determination. I had to admit to myself that I was afraid. I had to hold on to the hope that my husband would get better, and without fear, I needed to face a possibly bleak future.

I've always known that fear is a compelling emotion, a double-edged sword. It can be a motivational tool, propelling us to overcome challenging moments. Still, it can also be a paralyzing force, limiting our potential. Like a shadow, it follows you, obscuring the light of positivity and faith.

I was in a cloudy place in my life, praying for clarity. Facing the future is always an unknown period in everyone's life. Every step felt like a blind leap into the abyss of uncertainty. The man I had loved and respected for more than thirty years, the man who became my husband and our son's father, passed away four days after my fifty-fifth birthday. We were co-owners and managers of a multimillion-dollar business. He was the wind beneath my wings, the one person whose death I never imagined could come so soon. This was true but inconceivable.

So now what? How do you go from dancing the night away to planning a funeral a few months later? How do you reconcile the surreal contradiction of the celebration of life and the mourning of death? The first thing I had to do was to remind myself that on this road called life, "shit happens," and when it happens, we must clean it and move on. Much like how a turtle sheds its old shell to grow, I knew I needed to shed my grief to heal. Failure to clean it can become detrimental. By now, it was becoming clear by the minute that I must take the good with the bad, sometimes even smile when I was sad, and never forget what I had and still have.

So, I asked God, "Why? Why me? Why my Keith?" And God answered, "I sent him into your life for a season, and his time has come." The echo of His words was both a gentle balm and a sharp sting to my aching heart. In the quietude, I found myself turning to the wisdom of the turtle, patient, enduring, and silently moving forward despite its trials.

In my nursing school days, I recall having to memorize the five stages of grief—a theory developed by Dr. Elisabeth Kubler-Ross, a very famous Swiss American psychiatrist. While working with families at the hospice unit of my nursing home, I applied Dr. Kubler-Ross's grief theory to bereavement classes that I taught. I was familiar with and could even recite those stages in my sleep. Yet, they remained abstract concepts in light of the raw, visceral emotion I was now experiencing. Ironically, I found myself in an unexpected predicament, unable to escape the very grief I'd been teaching others to cope with. Slowly I realized that the shoe was on the other foot: this time, I was in pain; I needed grief counseling.

The first stage of grief is denial. As a nurse and healthcare professional, I accepted the fact of my husband's death. But while there was no denial in that sense, I found myself stuck, frozen in the next steps, grappling with the reality of life without him, a subtle form of denial that contradicted everything I had taught my patients' families. Teaching it and living through it are two different emotional experiences when dealing with grief. Unfortunately, I had no time to feel sorry for myself. Due to my Chief Executive Officer's responsibilities in the business, I could not stop because I had a dead husband. Life must go on. And the relentless march of time was my unyielding companion. Resilience, a turtle's unspoken motto, became my mantra as I waded through the murky waters of grief and responsibility.

I had to put on my big girl panties to move this colossal mountain I was facing. I was, however, fully confident that I had the fortitude to overcome such obstacles. At fifty-five, I knew that I had many challenges still to conquer. I had to learn to navigate independently; I no longer had Keith's guidance to rely on. The path ahead was fraught with hurdles, but I was ready to face them head-on. I was responsible for over five hundred beds in the nursing homes, over four hundred clients in a home care agency business, and a nursing school with an average of five hundred to eight hundred students. People's lives were in my hands. I had no time to feel sorry for myself, nor did I know how to move forward. I was in an approach and avoidance situation. I had to go to work; life must go on, yet all I wanted to do was stay in bed and cover my head with the sheets. Like a turtle, I would carry my home—my strength and willpower—on my back and walk steadfastly toward the horizon of hope.

I was lucky to have a son, then twenty-five years old, who was both an employee in our business and a personal force in my life, a stalwart pillar of support and a source of sage advice in my periods of doubt. I recall one particular moment as I was sitting in my husband's closet, holding and smelling his clothes. Keith's scent still lingered, a harsh reminder of his absence. It was then that Kevin walked in. He looked at me in shock and pity, his eyes brimming with empathy, yet firm with resolve. He extended his hands to help me off the floor, saying, "Mom, you have got to get your life together." Firmly he added, "You are not the first woman to have lost a husband, and I am sure you will not be the last. The nursing home residents need you; the staff needs you; and, Mom, I need you."

Despite his youth, my son showed an innate understanding of the business world, stepping into the role of vice president with mature ease and a commitment I hadn't expected. His invaluable expertise, sharpened by a master's degree in business and a law degree from George Washington University, was a breath of fresh air in our company. His credentials were impressive, but his character—kind, confident, patient, yet ambitious—truly set him apart. With a lot of grace and compassion for the seniors and staff, he grew up in the business to fill his father's shoes. Though different in shape, his footprints were no less effective in leading the company. He became my business partner, trustee, go-to person, and the company's president until the business was sold in 2018.

At work, I ceased to be "Mom" and became SV, as he began calling me in the office. This new title marked a shift in our relationship—we were now professional equals, our bond marked by a respectful distance, yet deepened by shared goals. I gained a partner, and I lost a son. We never regained the mother-son type of relationship, which I miss; yet, we remain as close as two partners made only in heaven. Our bond, transformed by circumstance, was no less intense. He blessed me with three handsome grandsons who affectionately call me "Nana." Additionally, my beautiful daughter-in-law entered our lives. Through her, I have been able to experience a unique mother-daughter relationship.

Luck has always played a significant role in my life. It arrived often and in the most surprising forms, like a giddy, unexpected guest. Some people call those moments a blessing; others believe a spirit of some sort is responsible for the good deeds that happened in their lives. Whatever we call it, those moments are special. They shimmer in our memory, their brightness never dimming. They have a way of leaving us in awe. We must simply exercise patience. In time, our luck will reveal itself.

Unfortunately, some people are so negative that they can't see good deeds even when it is right in front of their eyes. They refuse to look up and witness the beauty of the sky, choosing instead to wallow in their despair. I've realized that as we age, we accumulate wisdom—a golden treasure chest of lessons and insights, hard-earned and priceless. I came to appreciate that within every adverse event, there is always a silver lining peeking from behind the storm clouds, teasing us to chase it. Much like how a turtle appreciates the shelter its shell provides during a storm, it is up to me to identify the positive, highlight it and capitalize on it.

I once asked God why he took Keith away from me at such an inopportune time, He answered, "I gave you a son who is well prepared to fit into his father's shoes." It was a bitter pill to swallow, a truth too stark to ignore. Amid doubt and sadness, my faith and belief held me steady, providing comfort and a sense of purpose during the hardest times. They were my twin beacons in the night, guiding me toward acceptance. I quickly learned from God's answer that there is a reaction to every action. From every loss, there is a gain. Hope sprouts from the ashes of sorrow like a resilient sapling amidst the charred remnants. Sometimes, when events happen, we ask, "Why?" We may not receive the answer immediately, as God works in mysterious ways and in His own time. However, I also learned if we wait long enough, the answer will reveal itself. Like a sunrise after a long night, it arrives with quiet certainty. Like a turtle finally reaching the water after a long, arduous journey on the sand. We only need to believe, have faith, and pray to see and act accordingly at the right time.

Fear can often paralyze us, rendering us seemingly useless in facing challenges. However, the alternatives, belief in a higher power and self-belief, can provide a lifeline under even the most difficult circumstances. They act as defenses against the piercing arrows of uncertainty and doubt. Trust in yourself, faith in your God—whoever this spiritual being might be to you. Having the ability to hear that inner voice of wisdom and, when you indeed hear it, having the courage to act on it is a gift. It's like possessing a compass in the wilderness, guiding you through the unknown. Do not ignore it; just run with it.

In the face of these challenges, my gaze remained firmly fixed ahead. Rather than dwelling on the past, I moved from dream to action. I'm not one to look back; forward is the only direction I know, the only path I tread. Like a turtle reaching for the next blade of grass, I continually stretch beyond my comfort zone, moving forward with every effort. When I was an executive, a staff person often asked, "Don't you sleep at night?" Only because I would frequently come to work with a new idea, a new project, or a new way we could make life better for the nursing home residents and the staff who cared for them. My mind was a whirling dervish of thoughts, constantly churning out fresh ideas. I was never a procrastinator. I did not succumb to the brain's negative whispers, the inner voice of doubt trying to convince us that we cannot achieve. As I grew older, inside of me, I was still that spirited child with boundless energy, forever daring myself to climb or move one mountain after another. Age, in truth, holds no power over the spirit. And in my case, it seemed each passing year only stoked the fire within me, strengthening my core, much like a turtle's spirit that strengthens with each wave it overcomes.

Turtle Wisdom: The Power of Resilience

Take a moment and consider the humble turtle, a symbol of steadfastness and perseverance in many cultures. This chapter reflects that indomitable spirit, tracing the contours of a personal journey marked by profound loss, summoned strength, and a resilient spirit. It's about the embodiment of the turtle's slow, deliberate pace and unyielding determination—attributes that inspired my tenacity in the face of grief and adversity after Keith's passing.

The life of a turtle is far from simple. Imagine the world through a turtle's eyes. Each day is an obstacle course fraught with ravenous predators, treacherous landscapes, and the capriciousness of Mother Nature. Yet, despite these formidable challenges, turtles never retreat. They soldier on, forging ahead with a quiet, undeterred strength that's inspiring. In its unpredictable rhythm, life can sometimes land a devastating blow, a loss so profound that picking up the shattered pieces and moving forward can feel insurmountable, not just for your own sake but also for those who look to you for guidance and support. However, by taking a cue from the unwavering turtle, you too may exhibit fortitude by taking one cautious step at a time, continually marching forward.

In life, we all face our valleys and peaks, moments of despair interspersed with times of triumph. We traverse through stormy seasons, endure heart-wrenching tragedies, and navigate those rocky, difficult patches. But during these trying times, let's remember the steadfast resolve of the turtle—it stands as a living testament that no matter the size or severity of the hurdles we encounter, we possess the capacity to delve deep within ourselves and summon the strength to persevere. Whether in our professional endeavors or personal lives, the ability to hang tough, to resist the alluring temptation of surrender, is a quality that lies dormant within us all, ready to be awakened. The world may occasionally seem like a tumultuous sea, tossing us about in its unrelenting waves. Still, we harbor the power to brave these turbulent waters, facing adversity head-on, just like our friend, the turtle, does. With a shell as our armor and perseverance as our compass, we, too, can navigate the turbulent ocean of life.

TURTLE INSIGHTS

1. Can you recall a towering obstacle, a mountain you've had to climb? Perhaps it was a physical challenge, an emotional struggle, or a grueling endeavor in your career. How did you surmount it? Sometimes, to appreciate our growth, we must glance over our shoulders at the rocky path we've traversed.

2. How do you perceive resilience? Is it an inherent trait, as natural to you as breathing, or a quality you're still diligently honing, like a sculptor meticulously chipping away at a block of marble? Remember, there's no universal blueprint for resilience; it's a deeply personal journey as unique as our fingerprints.

3. Casting your mind back over the tapestry of your life, can you pinpoint an instance where you embodied resilience? A moment when the world seemed to conspire against you, yet you pushed on with the determination of a turtle inching steadily forward, regardless of the rocky terrain ahead?

4. In your current life scenario, how can you foster more resilience? Often, resilience is akin to a muscle—it grows stronger with every challenge we face, with each adversity we overcome. Like a blacksmith tempering steel, each blow life gives us shapes our resilience, making us more robust and capable.

5. Can you glean any wisdom nuggets from the turtle's unyielding approach? Slow and steady doesn't equate to weakness or passivity. It's a testament to unwavering determination, to the tenacity that refuses to give up, no matter how formidable the journey ahead appears. Like the turtle, we too can embody this perseverance, steadily making our way forward, one determined step at a time.

AFFIRMATIONS

- I have the strength and resilience to face life's challenges.

- Like the turtle, I will keep moving forward, no matter the obstacles.

- My past struggles have shaped me; I am stronger because of them.

- I trust my inner wisdom and courage to guide me through life's trials.

- I grow more resilient daily, embracing life's journey with grace and persistence.

CHAPTER TWO

Aging Backwards into a World of Technology

I arrived in America as a teenager in the mid-1960s from Port-au-Prince, Haiti, speaking very little English, if any, with a very strong French accent. After a rough beginning, I quickly learned that while we are all born into one world, our experiences make our individual realities vastly different. Under the glittering city lights of America, amidst its symphony of different languages, cultures, and dreams, I understood that I had to create my own rules if I were to make it and survive in America.

I worked as a seamstress in factories in New York City's Garment District for a while at the age of nineteen. I was later hired to be a nanny for a lovely caucasian family for several years. I then worked as a nursing assistant in a hospital nursery before enrolling in nursing school. I became a Licensed Practical Nurse, a Registered Nurse with a diploma from Manhattan State Hospital School of Nursing in New York, and a Professional Nurse with a master's degree in Health Services Administration from Georgetown University in Washington, D.C.

I was awarded a doctoral degree in Humane Letters at Voorhees College in South Carolina.

VOORHEES COLLEGE IN SOUTH CAROLINA

From a humble nursing assistant to a registered nurse, and eventually the owner of a major healthcare business in Washington, D.C., I climbed every rung of the nursing ladder.

But life, like a dance, is subject to constant changes in rhythm. Soon, the familiar beat of my life started to quicken. Life was perfect until the world that I thought I finally conquered started to metamorphose in front of my eyes. Like a turtle suddenly finding itself in the middle of a fast-paced highway, I also felt a jolt of the unfamiliar. I was no longer free. I was now attached to a beeper at my waist and connected as the beacon of every local and national organization and government agency, and yes, this included the nursing homes my company managed.

"I WAS NOW ATTACHED TO A BEEPER AT MY WAIST..."

Like a heartbeat keeping time, I was tethered to the pulse of my nursing homes, always available, always connected. Twenty-four hours a day, seven days a week. When I got beeped, I had to stop to find a telephone at a gas station, a store, or a phone booth on the side of a highway to call the nursing home.

A PHONE BOOTH ON THE SIDE OF A HIGHWAY

It was as though I was a turtle forced to interrupt its slow and steady progress, hurrying and scurrying like a hare instead, trying to catch up with the world whizzing by.

My beeper became an echoing reminder of the world's accelerating pace, a symbol of dependency. I was a turtle bearing a load that both protected and hindered me, slowing my pace yet keeping me tied to the fast-paced environment around me. In addition to the inconvenience of having to find a telephone to return the call, I discovered that the staff was becoming dependent on me. The employees stopped thinking and making decisions on their own. Whatever they needed, they beeped me because it was easy.

Despite working for myself, I was not a happy camper. At one of our corporate board meetings, I complained about this beeper constantly bothering me, even while I was sleeping. One of my partners, Victor, thought it would be better if I had a phone in my car. At that time, I was not aware that this technology even existed. Before long, like a strange alien creature, a phone was installed in my tiny two-seater BMW. Each addition felt like a new layer being added to my shell, transforming me further, much like a turtle adjusting to its expanding carapace.

The phone, mounted on the driver's side console, took up considerable space, crowding my driving leg. It was not just any phone; it was bulky (humongous!)—the largest telephone I had ever seen.

A monstrosity. A behemoth that resembled a suitcase more than a communication device.

When I complained of the discomfort of having that big awkward telephone near my driving leg, my partner Victor once again said, "Well, Solanges, why don't you get a Mercedes-Benz?"

"The Benz is a bigger car," he continued. "It will have more space for your phone. You are working so hard and doing such a great job with the company. I will motion that you get a company car. You deserve it." The motion passed: Our company, VMT Long Term Care Management Inc., would lease a Mercedes Benz with a telephone for Solanges to drive. The turtle had finally found a bigger shell.

And so, I found myself in a dream made real, navigating the winding roads of Washington, D.C. in the driver's seat of a gleaming Mercedes Benz. Go figure, this little skinny Haitian girl driving this big, gigantic Mercedes Benz in the early nineteen nineties all over Washington, D.C. Being positively noticed and appreciated for making millions of sacrifices to keep this business afloat was a sign that doing good work and being a role model to others has its perks. I was now the turtle who had found her rhythm amidst the chaos.

But life has a way of casting shadows into the brightest moments. Being too visible can also yield some unpleasant experiences. A memory unfolds, and I'm suddenly back in time. I recall driving this car in Maryland with my young son Kevin and his little friend William in the back seat. Our laughter echoed in the car, a happy tune in the background of an ordinary day. We were heading to summer camp at North Carolina State University, where the boys would be playing basketball with Coach Jimmy Valvano. Waiting patiently at a light, I made a legal left turn as the light turned green. Suddenly, I heard the police siren, the sound cutting through the air like a sharp knife. I looked in my rearview mirror, and sure enough, I was being followed—a turtle out of its comfort zone, crossing paths with a marauder.

As expected, I pulled over and stopped the car. My heart pounded in my chest, a drum echoing my rising apprehension. I was stunned as to why I was being stopped. The police officer exited his car and approached me, his silhouette looming like a predator's shadow over a sunlit beach, making even the bravest turtle apprehensive. As I turned the window down to greet the officer, I reassured the boys by asking them not to worry; we would be fine. The words were as much for me as they were for them. He requested my license and car registration. I complied. The familiar cards slipped from my hands into his, their importance magnified in this moment. He then sat in his car for the longest time until he finally returned, handed me my license with the registration, and matter-of-factly said, "You may go now." He gave me no tickets and no warning.

Being assertive and non-confrontational, I said, "Officer, may I ask why you stopped me?"

He replied, "I could not read your license plate."

I said, "So does that mean I will be stopped again between here and North Carolina, where I'm headed?"

He replied, "Ma'am, I don't know what other officers will do, but I would advise you just to go your merry way." In other words, be lucky I did not give you a ticket, arrest you—or worse.

I said, "Thank you, sir," and left.

Each word, each interaction in this encounter, remains a vivid snapshot in the album of my life. Like a turtle's journey through a stormy sea, every wave, every current, every droplet seems etched in my memory. These unlawful car stops were prevalent in the District of Columbia, Maryland, and Virginia, where we lived in the early 1980s. It was nothing more than harassment for him to stop me. I was a black woman with long braids driving a brand-new Mercedes Benz with a temporary license plate. I felt like prey, a target to be taken out and either imprisoned or killed. But as a turtle protecting itself in its shell, I carried my dignity and courage—

they acted as a vital shield. There has long been a history of black people experiencing intimidation by law enforcement. This regrettable fact, which hung heavily and oppressively in the air and went unacknowledged for years, was an unpleasant reality. Sadly, a lot of people have met their demise because of their ignorance of the fact that cops have a pad, pen, gun, and taser, and the capacity to conceal their misconduct.

I taught my son to remember that he has his life to lose and that only he can protect it—a difficult but necessary lesson wrapped in a mother's love and concern. Like a mother turtle laying her eggs on the shore and leaving them to the mercy of the world, I imparted to him the wisdom to survive and thrive in a sometimes unforgiving America. Racial profiling, as exemplified by the tragic death of Emmett Till decades ago, has always been real. It is still viciously practiced in America, as we have witnessed most recently in the death of George Floyd, Breonna Taylor, and many young black men and women, too numerous to cite in this book.

Once the storm of the Maryland incident passed, the sun of relief and happiness finally dared to shine. I had a wonderful time in the Carolinas. Kevin stayed with my girlfriend Gloria, William's mom, for the rest of the summer, and I traveled back safely to Washington, D.C. The journey back was filled with thoughts of the carefree summer days ahead. It was a special child-free summer where Keith and I were again free to fully enjoy each other in our beautiful home without any mommy and daddy interruptions.

Memories of my childhood—playing hide and seek with my siblings, baking with my mother, our noisy dinners—danced in my mind. I grew up in a large family of thirteen children, with my parents and a few helpers around the house. I have always wanted a big family of my own. I missed the sound of laughter, conversation, and movement in my own house. I had no idea how much even one child might strain a parent's relationship. I often marveled at how strong my parents must have been to raise thirteen kids.

Love, as I learned, sometimes needs to adapt to the hard truths and challenges of life. My husband Keith never wanted to have children, even though he turned out to be the perfect father. As for me, once I realized the effect of having children while striving to improve our lives socio-economically, I concluded that one child was enough—the reality, a bitter pill swallowed with a heavy heart. I could not wait to have a tubal ligation, making sure that getting pregnant was not an option.

Technological advancements seeped into our lives, unveiling a world of unforeseen possibilities. Just as a turtle adapts to changing landscapes, I adjusted to this new technological era. By now, I had a new electronic toy, a flip phone, and a new Benz with no bulky telephone. There was a time when owning devices like beepers, car phones, and, later, flip phones, often led people to assume you were a doctor, nurse, or, intriguingly, a drug dealer. But before long, this little tiny flip phone was becoming very popular. It was no longer a device used mainly by healthcare professionals.

"BY NOW, I HAD A NEW ELECTRONIC TOY, A FLIP PHONE."

The surge of technology, much like a high tide, reshaped our familiar landscapes, forcing us to adapt to a changing world. Visions of numbers and calculations appeared in my mind. In addition to flip phones, another electronic device that had become popular was a handheld calculator.

It was a big deal when I gifted my husband a small desktop calculator for Christmas. But before long, every woman's pocketbook had a small calculator. The sweet sound of keys clicking away became familiar in every home and office. The electronic world had arrived with a vengeance, forcing us to figure out how to adapt or be left behind.

Like a turtle embracing the shifting currents, I was ready to ride this whirling wave of technological change. Technology evolved so quickly that it affected every facet of our existence, fast-forwarding us into an unexpected explosion. The field of computers had officially entered the healthcare industry—an incursion into the future, an opening to opportunities. I was familiar with computers since my son's kindergarten class at Lafayette Elementary School received large desktop computers from IBM as part of an experiment called "Writing to Read."

Each child received a computer—not to take home because parents like us would not have known its usefulness nor how to operate the equipment; the computers remained in the classroom and were used daily under the teacher's supervision and instructions. The students, tiny visionaries charting a path toward a digitized future, created a nice booklet at the end of the program. And my baby boy, a kindergartner, designed the booklet cover, his little fingers crafting symbols of progress. This was the extent of my computer knowledge.

As for my late husband Keith, the digital realm was a playground where he thrived. As a systems analyst, he was experienced in working with mainframe computers.

These massive, formidable monsters could never possibly fit on a typical desktop. They were the titans of their time, humming in the heart of large organizations. They took on the herculean tasks of bulk data processing for things like census data, in-depth industry consumer statistics, enterprise resource planning, and large-scale transaction processing.

As an executive in healthcare, I observed how the proliferation of desktop computers started to creep in. They first appeared in the sterile environment of acute care hospitals, and years later, gradually made their way into the nursing homes industry. An optimist, I quickly realized these new machines' potential. I grew fond of how they hummed and whirred, creating vast expanses of knowledge from simple keystrokes. I started to appreciate the technology, reveling in the crisp financial reports that I received from the finance department. I eagerly awaited the statistical charts from my department directors and administrative assistant. It was like having an all-knowing oracle right at my fingertips. By this time, I was getting the hang of it. It felt like I had a personal magician at my disposal—all I had to do was tell my administrative assistant what I needed, and voilà, it happened.

However, in my mind, the computer was for everyone but me. It was a tool, yes, a magical one even, but not for me to wield. I saw it as an excellent means for others to meet my executive needs but never considered it something I should work on. I had no desire to have a computer on my desk. I was the conductor of this orchestra, not one of the musicians. I was the executive; I had hundreds of staff and a host of computer-savvy nieces and nephews, so the computer was a tool for them, not for me.

This sentiment was common among executives in my age bracket, as we cherished the familiar click of a pen and the rustle of paper and remained dedicated to our file cabinets. I never mastered the art of typing on a typewriter.

When I was a young adult, computers were as foreign as spaceships. Back in my college days, when professors began rejecting handwritten essays, we transitioned to using typewriters for our assignments.

Throughout college, I paid for the then-luxury of having my work typed up. There was a professional typist whose full-time job was to serve as the intermediary between students, companies, and the written word. In those days, typists were the key-holders to the digital realm. One needed to know how to type to use a computer, and I did not. When my director of finance suggested installing a computer on my desk, I politely declined. My administrative assistant offered to teach me the ways of this new device. Still, I respectfully declined her offer as well.

Communication began to migrate from the tangible world of paper to the virtual world of "email." I found this shift unsettling. It felt like words were being sucked into a vortex, disappearing into a place I didn't understand. As an active member of the American Health Care Association and the District of Columbia Health Care Association, I was surprised when both announced that they would cease using the United States Postal Service for communication. All news and updates would be sent electronically via email. The digital revolution had arrived, and I was still holding onto my pen and paper. I felt that a small machine was slowly erasing me. However, I was at a crossroads; I needed to catch this technological train or be left behind.

Finally, out of sheer necessity, I relented and agreed to have a large-screen computer placed on my desk; this was when laptops, iPods, and cellphones were still a futuristic dream.

A "well-done" executive business leader is someone who leads in such a way that at the end of their lives, they will hear the words "well done" from the people who have watched them grow, worked with them, supervised them, and from the God whom they have worked to please. However, striving to become a well-done leader requires stamina and a can-do attitude that can use fear as a catalyst for change.

Just as a turtle must navigate its path regardless of the obstacles, I had to also confront my reluctance to embrace technology.

To remain a "well-done" leader, I understood that I couldn't cling to the ways of the past. I couldn't be a relic in a world racing toward the future. I needed to progress, adapt, and become a leader ready for tomorrow's challenges.

With typing being my Achilles' heel, the staff gifted me a voice recorder. It was a tiny piece of tech magic, a device that could translate my spoken words into typed text. I was supposed to speak to this device, and it would dictate my words onto the computer. However, the machine seemed to get lost in translation, unable to decipher my strong Haitian accent. The transcripts were nothing short of comedic. I couldn't help but laugh at the hilarious word salad it produced.

We all know that fear can be crippling; it's a hurdle that seems insurmountable. The survival of the fittest isn't about the strongest, but the most adaptable. Just as a turtle learns to adjust its course based on the obstacles it encounters, I also knew I had to be malleable and adaptable. It's a dance between being rigid and being flexible, and I knew I had to learn the steps. I realized I needed to use my fear as a stepping stone, a catalyst to conquer my apprehensions about computers, especially my inability to type. There's a saying that you can't teach an old dog new tricks. Well, I was that dog, ready and eager to learn the tricks of the digital trade.

Step by step, I taught myself to navigate the electronic landscape, learning this new language one keystroke at a time. I typed out my memoir, my fingers dancing across the keyboard, turning the pages of my handwritten notebooks into digital memories. As I got older, I became younger in the face of technology. I managed to age backward in this rapidly advancing world, keeping my status as a "well-done" leader.

Just like a turtle, keep moving forward. Consider how a turtle steadily advances, unimpeded by the weight of its shell, a symbol of resilience and adaptability. Use that image to encourage your progress. Because remember, a turtle can't move backward; it can only carry its shell and inch forward toward improvement.

The world of technology continues to spin at an alarming rate, but my fear of it has diminished. My initial apprehension has blossomed into curiosity, my earlier trepidation now fuels a drive for exploration. And like the turtle that has reached the other side of the field, I've made it through my journey, arriving at a place of understanding and acceptance. I've ventured down various technological pathways, dabbling in every social media platform, partaking in lively chat room discussions, leading Zoom presentations, and even dipping my toes into the waters of artificial intelligence (AI). I've become a digital explorer, charting my course in this electronic age.

Turtle Wisdom: Adaptation is Key

Turtles, those quiet, sturdy creatures, have roamed the Earth for an astounding 200 million years or more, outlasting the dinosaurs and carving a path through time that few other species can claim. These ancient creatures, who have witnessed epochs come and go, hold within them a tale of survival, tenacity, and adaptation. Their shells carry the history of their evolution, each groove and ridge an account of a time weathered, an obstacle overcome.

Just as these resilient creatures have navigated the eons, my journey, detailed in this chapter, tells a similar tale of adaptation and growth. It's a saga woven with the threads of navigating unfamiliar physical and technological territories. I was a stranger in a new country, adjusting to an alien culture that was a world away from what I knew. Alongside this personal evolution, I grappled with a seismic shift in a different realm, the relentless march of technology.

Picture a turtle on a beach, facing a vast, unknown ocean. It doesn't balk or retreat; it plunges forward, undeterred by the waves that could wash it away. I found myself on a similar beach, looking at the immense sea of technology, its waves threatening to sweep me off my feet. But like the turtle, I chose to swim, adapt, and evolve.

But the lesson of the turtle isn't exclusive to me or those ancient creatures. It's a universal truth that extends to each one of us. The world spins on the axis of change, and every rotation brings something new, something different. Our lives are in constant flux, and the pace of change is like a swift current that could easily carry us away if we aren't prepared.

In this rapid current of change, our ability to adapt becomes our life jacket. It keeps us afloat, ensuring we don't get swept away. Whether it's adjusting to a new role at work, acclimating to a new city's rhythm, or learning to navigate the labyrinth of technology, our adaptability dictates our survival and success. In these uncertain waters, resisting change is like swimming against the current; it drains our energy and gets us nowhere. On the other hand, embracing change allows us to use the current to propel us forward, transforming challenges into stepping stones that lead to new opportunities.

So, let's be like the turtle. Let's carry our homes—our sense of self—within us and face each wave of change with determination and grace. Because, like the turtle, we are built to adapt, evolve, and thrive, no matter what seas we must navigate.

TURTLE INSIGHTS

1. **Reflect on your Journey of Adaptation:** Take a moment to think back to a time when you had to adapt to a significant change in your life. Was it a job shift, a move to a new city, a family expansion, or even something as mundane as learning a new phone system? How did you handle the transition? What emotions surfaced, and how did you address them? Reflecting on these experiences provides insights into how you react to change and strategies that can be helpful in future transitions.

2. **Resistance to Modernity:** We've all experienced hesitance with new technology or environmental changes. Maybe it's the latest smartphone, new software at work, or even the idea of a self-

driving car. What modern innovations are you finding hard to embrace? Identify them and consider why you're resisting. Then, create a plan to familiarize yourself with these changes gradually. The goal is not to become an expert overnight but to foster a mindset of openness and adaptability.

3. **Embracing Persistence and Adaptability:** My journey to technological literacy was not a straight line but a testament to persistence and adaptability. How can you integrate this approach into your life? Is it a new language you want to learn? A fitness goal you aim to reach? Maybe a new career path you're carving out? Apply the same tenacity and willingness to adapt as you navigate these pursuits.

4. **Adaptability Role Models:** Each of us can likely identify a person in our life who embodies adaptability. They could be as close as a family member or as famous as a world-renowned entrepreneur. What makes them adaptable? Is it their curiosity, resilience, or their perpetual optimism? Once you've identified these traits, consider ways to emulate them in your own life.

5. **Areas of Adaptability:** Finally, introspect on your adaptability spectrum. Where do you display a chameleon's knack for blending in, and where do you feel like a stubborn mule refusing to move? Once you have a clear picture, create a plan to nurture adaptability in those rigid areas. Remember, this isn't about a complete overhaul but gradual changes leading to a more flexible you.

AFFIRMATION

- I welcome change with open arms, seeing it not as an obstacle but as a stepping stone for growth.

- Like the steadfast turtle, my journey may be slow-paced, but it is always forward-moving. I adapt to my surroundings, evolving with every step I take.

- My resilience is a testament to my flexibility. No matter the circumstance, I can thrive, adapt, and conquer.

- Every past success in adapting to new situations fuels my confidence for future changes. I look back not with fear but with a sense of accomplishment.

- I am on a constant quest for personal growth and learning, understanding that adaptability is the compass that will guide me to success.

CHAPTER THREE

Dared to Be

Life challenges are fertile ground for success. From birth until death, we continuously change—growing in some areas, like wisdom and stoutheartedness, while other aspects of our health might decline. Just like a baby sea turtle hatching from its egg, we emerge into the world, naked and vulnerable yet filled with a potent instinct for survival. Granted, we may not have a choice about how our life begins; however, like a turtle bearing its shell, we are responsible for how we spend the rest of the time we are given. Some will succeed because they are *destined* to succeed, due to favorable circumstances, but most will succeed only because they are *determined* to succeed, their grit and their tenacity akin to that of a turtle hauling its heavy shell over uneven terrain. I firmly believe that most successes are the product of motivation, perseverance, and the ability to seize opportunities when they present themselves. We should be like the turtle—steadily make our way across the beach, undeterred by the vastness of the ocean that awaits us.

Imagine if a newborn baby could express their struggles. Their experiences with learning to roll over or waiting for nourishment would be enlightening; they would voice the difficulties inherent to learning to crawl, walk, run, and the inability to clean oneself when soiled. Each breathless sigh, every triumphant giggle, and the endless cycle of trial and error that leads to victory—certainly, the insights from such experiences would offer profound perspectives on resilience and growth. Only babies know of those early life challenges, a world hidden away under gurgles and giggles.

As a teenager, I cared for two nieces from birth until their toddler years, watching as they blossomed from helpless infants into eager explorers, their transformation as captivating as witnessing a turtle hatchling grow into a mature, wise turtle. Later, I worked in a caucasian household caring for two children, a three-year-old girl and a one-year-old boy. Soon afterward, another little girl was born. I was her caregiver from birth until I left that employment. With that life experience, I can attest to having some knowledge of growth and development even before my formal nursing school education.

In addition to my expertise in early childhood development, I was fortunate to have spent forty-two years of my professional life caring for the elderly in hospitals, nursing homes, and their community home. Just like a turtle carrying its home on its back, seniors carry decades of life experiences with them, each one a testament to their endurance. Caring for seniors, with their multifaceted needs and conditions, can be more complex, challenging, and demanding than caring for an infant—a labyrinth of needs and wants that continually morphs and transforms, as varied and unpredictable as the patterns on a turtle's shell. It has been said, "Once a man, twice a child." It's a concept that I thoroughly disagree with and feel qualified to defend. Particular needs may appear to be the same. However, lifting and carrying a baby on one's shoulder is far less taxing than lifting, from a bed to a wheelchair, a cognitively diminished, physically impaired stroke victim. Even changing a senior's position in bed is more taxing than changing a baby's diaper.

So, what is aging anyway? In the grand tapestry of life, we start to age from the day we are born. We don't suddenly wake up and realize that we have lived on this earth for several days, months, and years—and that we are old. Each day that passes, we are a day older, our journey shaping us, molding us into sculptures of time. And we've left behind a day that we will never relive. Therefore, life consists of a series of mountains we must climb from birth to death. Each time we reach the top of a mountain, we are faced with another mountain to climb. To reach the peak of our next mountain, we must first descend to the valley of life and start at the very base of our next mountain.

Oh, how we remember the jubilance of our high school graduation only to start as a freshman in college. This scenario continues throughout life. In the Caribbean, we say, "Behind every mountain is another mountain." Behind every life achievement is another milestone to conquer. A baby cannot verbalize the pain and the difficulties of climbing life's mountains. On the other hand, seniors painfully suffer and know the height of each mountain they've climbed. Those are the burdens that come with the blessings of aging.

From my forty-two years as a geriatric health care professional, I can testify to the immense challenges of caring for a disabled senior. While I acknowledge that every area of healthcare has its own complexities, including pediatric care, my experiences have led me to this personal conclusion. Those hurdles are what prepare us for the obstacles we will face once we reach the workforce, married life, parenting and caring for one's own elderly parents.

I entered the long-term care industry as a thirty-one-year-old nurse and retired at the age of seventy-one. Each day, I felt blessed for my own health and independence, particularly when I saw many women much younger than me bound to their nursing home beds. Some sat all day in a wheelchair, wondering why they were still alive when there was no longer any quality in living. Some were the lone survivors of their families, having no blood relatives left. I cared for women who came to Washington, D.C., to work, never married, and had no children or family in the area. Some women affected by cancer, multiple sclerosis, or drug abuse were younger than me; many could have been me. Sometimes, I would observe them and be overcome by empathy, pondering the complexities of life. In these moments, I would find myself reflecting on my own career choice. Why, among all possible paths in healthcare, had I found my calling in end-of-life care? Yet, amidst this uncertainty, a reaffirming voice within me would respond, "Why not you?" Each time I questioned myself, the desire to hang in there became stronger and stronger.

Working with seniors is taxing physically and mentally, and yet very rewarding. Each smile they give you is like a precious gem in a treasure trove. Those seniors were my friends, mother, father, and ancestors. I was repeatedly asked, "How do you stay so motivated in this line of work?"

As painful as this business could be, I had such love for what I was doing that I did not even realize that forty-plus years had passed; I was growing older and becoming a senior myself. So, I asked Solanges, the girl in the mirror, "What kind of senior do you want to be?" And my inner voice, as consistent as ever, answered with conviction, "One Who Dared to Be."

I was determined to rewrite the rules of aging to be different from what I lived through in my work experience, and my heart was ablaze with a thirst for change. I yearned for something different, not only for myself but also as an example for others. I envisioned an aging process filled with joy, exploration, dignity, elegance, and insight. I wanted to age as a turtle does, with grace and wisdom, carrying my life's journey with me, but not allowing it to weigh me down. I wanted to be a role model for others and share my experience to empower women. So what did I do? I started to date a prominent lawyer who was my junior by a few years, his charisma and intelligence like a splash of vibrant paint across a blank canvas. I sold my business, published my memoir, and embraced a zest of enduring youthfulness—becoming a woman who, like a Toys "R" Us kid with an ever-ready battery, refused to let her spirit grow old. I embraced my inner vibrancy, never losing my sense of wonder and enthusiasm, each day an adventure waiting to be had, each moment a memory waiting to be crafted. In my heart, I knew that while my body may age, like the ageless spirit of a turtle, my spirit would remain eternally young.

Turtle Wisdom: Embrace Change and Aging with Grace

There is something inherently beautiful about the turtle's journey through life, gracefully transitioning from a tiny, vulnerable hatchling into a wise, resilient creature, fully equipped with the strength and wisdom amassed over years. This journey, though slow, is a testament to perseverance, patience, and the embracing of life's ever-changing seasons. Much like the turtle, our lives too unfold in stages, each phase replete with its unique set of challenges and opportunities to grow and evolve.

Life is not a race against time, but rather a pilgrimage, a steady, determined trek brimming with chances to learn, understand, and accumulate wisdom. It's not about reaching a specific age or benchmark but about how we travel through our unique journey, how we tackle our trials, and what lessons we draw from our experiences.

Aging, much like change, is a given—it's an unchanging truth as steady as the ebbing and flowing tides. Like the turtle, we all age, undergoing physical and psychological transformations that can be intimidating. But, rather than fight against these inevitable alterations, we must embrace them, see them as part of the grand tapestry of life. By truly understanding and accepting the reality of aging, we can lead lives brimming with purpose and vigor, gaining wisdom and a sense of serenity from the process.

Aging doesn't have to be a downfall—it can be a ladder, an opportunity for continual growth and enlightenment. By shifting our perception, we can view aging as a chance to live our lives more profoundly, a window to grow old with the dignity and grace of a wise, old turtle.

TURTLE INSIGHTS

1. Perception shapes reality. How do you perceive aging, and how does this perception color your life's canvas?

2. Can you recall a moment when you, like a turtle, faced change or the process of aging head-on?

3. How might you translate the lessons from the turtle's unhurried journey into wisdom for your life's path?

4. What does aging with dignity and grace look like to you?

5. In what ways can you challenge the status quo and rewrite the conventional narrative of aging based on what you've witnessed so far?

AFFIRMATIONS

- I embrace change and aging with grace and wisdom, channeling the patience and perseverance of the turtle.

- I am as resilient and adaptable as a turtle, ready to face life's myriad of challenges.

- I celebrate the wisdom and experience garnered with each sunrise and sunset.

- Like a turtle, my journey is one of continuous growth and evolution, not confined by milestones or years.

- I honor and value the process of aging, viewing it not as a downfall but as a cherished privilege and an opportunity for continuous learning and growth.

CHAPTER FOUR

A Badass Girl

Why be a badass girl instead of a good little old lady? What pushed me to be this person rather than a quiet, traditional elder? Well, it was time for me, Solanges, to have some fun. I had made so many sacrifices throughout my life that I decided it was time to fall in love with myself and show myself what a good, fun life is all about. Like the steadfast journey of a turtle across a sandy shore, I took this new phase of life in stride, tasting the thrills of singledom with gusto. Each day was an uncharted beach, beckoning me to explore.

My husband died so young that he did not get to relish his retirement. He contributed to social security, retirement plans, and Medicare. Unfortunately, he did not get to enjoy the fruits of his labor. He did not get the chance to see the woman I had become, a journey he had greatly influenced and supported. Death deprived him of the chance to see our son become a lawyer, marry, and have children. I decided to enjoy, for me and him, the God-given days that are ahead.

I chose to live today and every day as though I knew it was my last. I promised to climb every mountain before me—to become a conqueror and not a victim of time. I decided to beat getting old. I decided to grow backward to rewrite the rules of growing older.

The joke in my family is, "When she dies, the inscription on her tombstone should read, *She Savored Every Moment.*" Once Keith was gone, I made it a point to work very hard since I no longer had him as my security blanket. However, for as hard as I was working, I played harder than I worked. Waiting to play after retirement is the biggest mistake that one can make. I call it not taking a sip of joy from the cup of life. Since we know tomorrow is not promised, why not enjoy every minute of today?

As the moon pulls the tide, creating a path for turtles to venture upon the beach, my time with Clifford created new paths for joy and discovery in my life. Just like a turtle, I didn't wait for a perfect day to set out on my journey. I chose to seize each day as an opportunity for new adventures. Enjoying life today is as precious as taking a last breath. I became single at fifty-five after being in a relationship for over thirty years. My best friend Ana became a widow eight months earlier, so we were two wild hot-blooded females with no husband and no children to care for. We were free to fly and fly. We did match.com, eHarmony, Ourtime, and others. Ana was like a butterfly; she was more of a social media user than I was. She would not stop until she got herself a man, and that she did! I tried it a few times but was never comfortable meeting a stranger at a restaurant.

Clifford was a surprise beacon in the vast ocean of life, an unexpected ally in my journey. Just about a year after my husband departed from my life, I met Clifford, who turned out to be the perfect person. Just as a turtle knows when to venture out of its shell, I recognized this perfect moment in Clifford. He was tall, dark, and handsome like my late husband; however, he was as crazy as I was. My Keith was conservative and pastel, a real British man from the island of Barbados. On the other hand, Clifford was a wild Black American man from Brooklyn, New York. They were both men who, like me, grew up from nothing to become well-educated individuals with a lot of class. They would open the car door and pull the chair for a lady. They were very knowledgeable about their wine and spoke proper English.

Despite his previous reputation as a player, who only wined and dined without commitment, Clifford fit perfectly into my life. It was as if he had been hoping and praying to find a woman like me, someone who could hold her own in every aspect of life—educational, social, and financial. A woman who would fit his decorum—someone with good taste, class, and beauty. He certainly knew how to appreciate a woman's worth.

For our first Valentine's celebration as a couple, he invited me to wine, dine and celebrate this momentous occasion at The Inn at Little Washington in Virginia.

"The Inn," as it is famously referred to, is the Valentine's Day celebration spot for lovers in our tri-state District of Columbia, Virginia, and Maryland. Ana and I always dreamed of being escorted and spending Valentine's night at The Inn one day. During our administrator days, we both were invited to dinner at The Inn by Allen, the owner of the company that insured our businesses. We were picked up in a long-stretched limousine equipped with a full bar and taken to The Inn at Little Washington. We left The Inn promising ourselves to return.

Each journey with Clifford was an unscripted exploration, a voyage into the thrilling unknown. He is a man who believes that he can run multiple roads at the same time. The constant tick-tock of the clock seemed to hold no sway over Clifford; his arrival times were as unpredictable as the weather. He had no respect for time—one of the behaviors that I had to learn to live with if I was to remain in this relationship. Yet, despite his ever-late arrivals, traveling with Clifford could be the best time ever. His tardiness was often a result of an impromptu detour—a charming antique shop or a roadside diner with incredible pies. It was a testament to his never-lost, childlike wonder. Our curiosity led us to make unexpected stops whenever we came across quaint towns or charming villages. Very often, the kid in us would come out, and it would take us longer to get to our destination because we stopped to play along the way. Much like a turtle knows the joy of unexpected finds in the vast ocean, Clifford and I cherished the surprises our trips offered.

The allure of The Inn was like a siren call promising beauty and serenity, a lantern in the dark leading us to tranquility. We finally arrived at The Inn Thursday afternoon for our Valentine's Day dinner and overnight stay. Even though it was my second visit to The Inn, it might as well have been considered my first. Perhaps it was Clifford's presence or my newfound joy, but it looked different. It had the calm allure of a secluded bay where turtles nest, a place that, even when frequented, always feels like a new discovery. Being there with Clifford was a wholly new experience—a tender interlude rather than a business meeting. I was in high heaven, like an eighteen-year-old, in love again.

Clifford's attitude toward Valentine's Day was like a technicolor movie compared to Keith's black-and-white outlook. During our thirty-plus years of marriage, Keith had never taken me away for Valentine's Day. To my British Caribbean man, Valentine's Day was created for business so vendors could sell flowers, chocolate, and cards. As such, he did not buy into this hoopla about Valentine. The most I recall getting was a beautiful card signed "Love, Keith." I assume he did it because he knew it would make me happy, not because he felt or believed in the celebration.

Clifford, on the other hand, embraced the spirit of the day like a headliner taking center stage, reveling in every beat of the moment. We looked around, breathed the air, and visited the gift shop before we even made our way to registration. We were both in awe that we were there. As he told me, he had always wanted this experience but had never found the right woman until me.

The cost of the celebration was steep, yet, like the entrance to an exclusive gala, it felt exhilarating rather than intimidating. It cost one thousand dollars per person for the Valentine's Day dinner, night stay, and breakfast in the morning. When we decided to go, we agreed to each pay for ourselves so that the trip wouldn't be a major expense for one of us.

Unbeknownst to Clifford, one of my "ladies' room" trips was actually to the front desk to clear the total bill before checking out. I moved like a whisper in the wind, as silently assertive and decisive as only age and wisdom can allow. I was becoming a different type of senior who is free to "do it her way," take risks and embrace the unexpected. I paid the whole bill not because I had to but because I wanted to, because I could, and because I was becoming a badass girl.

Our suite was a resplendent two-story haven, a stage set for romance with a charming, hanging indoor balcony that seemed straight out of a fairy tale.

When we opened the front door, we discovered a living room, a bar, a powder room, and a hanging balustrade. A long narrow staircase took us upstairs to the main bedroom and bathroom.

Captivated by the intoxicating spirit of the place, I was like a voyager encountering a new, beautiful land, thrilled by every alluring discovery. I quickly ran up the stairs to look down at Clifford, who was already at the bar opening a bottle of champagne that was cooling on ice.

In a flurry of anticipation, I slipped into my stunning red-and-white cocktail dress. I slid on my red pumps, heading to the beautifully decorated dining room for dinner. I felt invincible, ablaze with confidence, and primed for whatever life dared to throw at me.

A Book for Lovers was placed delicately on my seat, a Valentine's Day surprise from the establishment, a thoughtful gift for the fortunate ladies celebrating at The Inn. Oh, what a night it was! What a night! Clifford did not mince his words in the morning, playfully recounting out loud at breakfast the impulsive adventure (my "naughty behaviors") of our passion-infused evening. Certain garments were left strewn on the living room floor, evidence of our passion that couldn't wait for the upstairs bedroom.

The next morning was a sweet, slow awakening, the world outside the window sparkling like a precious jewel. The Inn served us an elegant and succulent breakfast, complete with mimosas. A single red rose adorned our table, which I added to the two dozen red roses Clifford had delivered to our suite.

Valentine's Day blossomed into a cherished tradition, an eagerly anticipated overnight escape to an exotic venue that ignited our senses and strengthened our bond. Being a partner at a law firm where vacations were virtually unheard of, Clifford was always the first in the office and the last to leave. We were in New York to celebrate Clifford's thirtieth anniversary with the firm. During the celebrations, Mr. Berstein personally thanked me, acknowledging the positive force I was in Clifford's life and appreciating my efforts in enticing him out of the office for vacations. It was an elegant gathering, and the whole weekend in New York was invigorating and a lot of fun. We covered the whole Central Park on a tandem bike.

At dinner, I shared an anecdote that involved Clifford, my Mr. Workaholic. During one of our trips to St Croix, this man worked on the phone for a whole day while we toured the business section of the island. I would walk into a museum or a store, and my man would be standing or sitting outside, talking on the phone the entire time. His dedication to his work was an unwavering flame, burning bright with obligation and ambition. While on a trip to Dubai and Abu Dhabi, we flew to the Seychelles Islands; this guy would wake up early, sit on the balcony of our villa, and work.

He did the same thing while in Jamaica, Greece, Chile, Barbados, and Haiti. He was always working.

While Clifford's dedication to his work was commendable, it often meant stolen moments and hasty goodbyes, like a wandering explorer setting off for uncharted lands.

Fortunately for him, I was a very busy businesswoman in my own right. I understood Clifford's need to stay connected to his work. Therefore, I ignored the behavior and enjoyed the moments and his companionship. I was in the company of someone that I admired and who made me happy. I could not believe how lucky I was to have met the perfect person to fill the void left by my late husband.

Christmas was a blend of old and new, tradition and innovation, like a modern remix of a classic song. Clifford and I would do the usual events at home with my son and his family. The kids would create their own ornaments for the tree, using our pictures. My daughter-in-law would get matching pajamas for everyone every year, making long-lasting, treasured memories.

The next day, we would travel to an exotic destination to bring in the New Year. We indulged in extravagant dinners at renowned wineries. Nestled in the heart of Napa Valley and along the lush banks of the Russian River, we savored some of the world's finest wines, guided by famous sommeliers. We traveled from one winery to another just to taste different varieties of wine. We always traveled with a chauffeur so that we could drink indiscriminately.

Clifford and I had grown attuned to each other's idiosyncrasies and needs, making our time together resonant and fulfilling. Oh, what exhilarating fun we had! How crazy we were! Laughter echoed around us, and our unabashed joy turned heads. Over the years, we danced our way into New Year's Eve in various corners of the world, from Valparaíso in Chile to Dubai and Australia, where dozens of cruise ships lined up for the fireworks.

For all our trips, Clifford was the organizer and the decision maker. His meticulous planning brought me to enchanting places I had never even heard of, such as the Seychelles Islands.

I recall one evening in Dubai when he surprised me with a dinner setting unlike any other. We were in the heart of the desert, the pitch-black darkness punctuated only by the flickering torches left behind by the hotel staff. A low-set table awaited us, impeccably arranged with everything necessary for a sumptuous five-course feast, complete with a bottle of Moët champagne.

As the van that dropped us off disappeared, leaving us with a promised return time, a blend of romantic allure and looming trepidation enveloped me. The vast expanse of the dark desert made our solitude even more palpable. Although I cherished the sentiment behind this unique experience, I silently vowed it would be a once-in-a-lifetime adventure. Still, I couldn't help but appreciate Clifford's thoughtfulness. There we were, just the two of us, isolated in the vastness of the desert under the canopy of a starlit sky.

From Dubai, where the scorching desert heat contrasted sharply with the city's cool, futuristic architecture, we embarked on a thrilling drive to Abu Dhabi. The journey was a feast for the senses, offering glimpses into the region's vibrant culture. We visited the mosque both during the day and at night to witness its magnificent allure. These religious edifices, opulently constructed and preserved, stand as treasured monuments. To enter, one must be appropriately attired, barefoot, and maintain reverent silence.

After days of immersing ourselves in its allure, we then boarded a plane to the Seychelles Islands. There, I had the mesmerizing opportunity to observe turtles in their natural habitat. Among them, we encountered a one-hundred-and-sixty-year-old creature of splendid grandeur.

Under the gentle sun, we fed the turtles; I danced in jubilation beside a special turtle who took a liking to me.

And, yes, we captured these unforgettable moments in numerous pictures. Now, in my senior years, I revisit each one of those journeys through videos, reliving the magic all over again.

On the way from the airport, I was shocked when I heard our driver speaking Creole. Clifford knew about the local language but waited for me to find out. The experience of hearing Creole spoken as a primary language in a country other than my native Haiti was truly memorable, bringing an unexpected touch of home to this foreign landscape. I would interact with the natives and pretend I was a Seychellois, but the accent always gave me away. Every moment was pure bliss, observing Clifford's quiet bewilderment and the endearing smile that never left his face as I carried on animated conversations with my newfound family.

As we traveled within the scenic landscapes of New Zealand, having journeyed from Australia, the driver broke our reverie with the announcement of a day-long excursion packed with exciting activities.

Clifford and I looked at each other when he mentioned a helicopter ride to experience landing on a glacier. Since we were both up for an adventure, we paid the fee and took the ride even though I was wearing flip-flops. Clifford and I were not afraid to step out of our comfort zones and dive into the unknown.

With Clifford, every moment held the potential for delightful surprises and spontaneous adventure, from impromptu dances in the rain to exhilarating midnight strolls along unfamiliar city streets.

The following year, we traveled to Saint Solange Village in France, where I shared the spiritual beauty of the town that means so much to me.

On various Caribbean trips, we turned our voyages into double dates, exploring the sights and sounds of Punta Cana in the Dominican Republic, the Jade Mountains in Saint Lucia, and my home country of Haiti, together with my son and his girlfriend.

As a couple, we attended their wedding in Barbados and always had big fun throughout our worldly traveling experiences alone or with family and friends.

For Clifford's birthday, I surprised him with a romantic cruise to Venice, Italy, where the melodious strains of a serenade filled the air as we glided in a gondola. We then flew to Greece and toured several Greek islands, like Santorini, Delos, and Mykonos.

We worked hard to check off the places we wanted to visit while financially stable and healthy. Clifford and I grew up with low to moderate means. Having found each other in our late fifties and early sixties, and fortunate enough to have ample funds to explore our desires, we complemented each other well. We were inseparable. In many ways, Clifford and I were akin to two turtles who, having spent years on solitary journeys, found each other late in life, now savoring the fruits of our labor and basking in the shared warmth of our connection.

Clifford's infectious humor and generous spirit quickly endeared him to my family and friends, making him an indispensable part of every gathering and celebration. Our journey took us beyond the bustling capital of Port-au-Prince, all the way to the enchanting province of Jacmel. Here, in the soul of Haiti, I had built a school that served the children of Meyer, Jacmel, from pre-Kindergarten through high school. It was there that I first introduced Clifford to that side of the country.

Our journey by car took us to the outskirts of Leogane, where civilization gave way to untouched nature. From here, we had to decide between walking through the difficult terrain for several exhausting hours or riding a local motorcycle down the dangerous paths. Given the perilous nature of the road and the significant distance ahead, we decided to hire a motorcycle driver. Unfortunately, this was where Clifford's unbridled sense of humor almost got us killed.

I was the center passenger between those two men on the bike. The driver instructed Clifford to move closer to me for balance, but my gentleman caller was unfamiliar with Creole, the local language. When I translated the directions from our driver, Clifford misinterpreted my intentions and thought I was teasing him; ever the mischief-maker, he saw this as an invitation for a more intimate contact during our bumpy journey. He started laughing at me uncontrollably in his usual playful way, saying, "What happened? You want to feel me?" In fact, we needed to balance our weight for the motorcycle to climb up the hill; the bike would flip over if most of the weight were toward the back end. His misunderstanding led him to dismiss my request, a decision with immediate and painful consequences. He was laughing without stopping, and the motorcycle flipped.

The three of us fell off the bike on top of a mountain. Luckily, we did not roll over, which could have been deadly. I was the only one with a significant injury. As we tumbled off the bike, I was unfortunate enough to land near the motorcycle's hot muffler, resulting in a painful third-degree burn on my right leg.

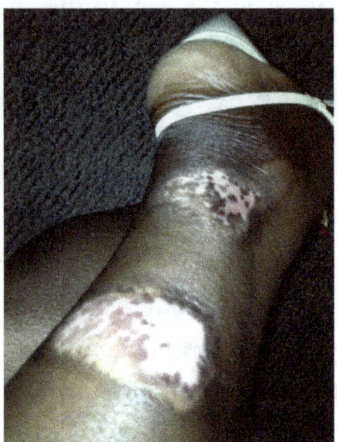

We were deep in a mountain where there were no doctors and no hospitals. By the third day, the cruel reality of my injury set in. The burns on my leg throbbed with a relentless, scorching pain, their inflamed edges hinting at a worrisome infection. It was clear that we had to leave Leogane. I flew back to Washington, D.C. I sat in a wheelchair at the airport and went straight to Kaiser Permanente. I was on crutches and unable to return to work for a few weeks.

I became a real badass girl in my senior years, after meeting my good old badass boy. I was convinced that age was indeed just a number accumulated from birth until we died. I also realized that I was one of the lucky ones. I was spared from chronic illnesses, which rob seniors of enjoying life. I was fortunate to have the means to support an exciting lifestyle.

Gratitude became my constant companion, and prayer a natural part of my daily routine. With faith as my anchor and Mother Mary as my guide,

I expressed my thankfulness to God for granting me these opportunities and sending me the perfect companion for the life journey I embarked upon. I enjoyed having the chance to experience that lifestyle to the fullest and never took it for granted. I prayed that I would always stay on the top of this fun-filled mountain.

Just as mountains are not smooth, life's journey is often filled with obstacles and challenges. The key, however, lies in recognizing opportunities and seizing them when they present themselves. It's like finding a foothold on a steep climb, offering the chance to push forward. If mountains were smooth, we would not have been able to climb them. I knew sooner or later I would find myself in a valley staring up at a new set of mountains to climb; some at times might appear too steep but still must be conquered. I had to get to the other side. Drawing from my own journey, I've come to firmly believe that Girls Can Move Mountains.

I knew this great style of living would end someday, as it did after more than thirty memorable years with my late husband, Keith. Much like a turtle that leaves a distinct trail in the sand, only for it to be washed away by the tides, I knew that every journey, however beautiful and fulfilling, would leave behind only memories and an ending.

Turtle Wisdom: Live Life with Audacity

Just like turtles that dare to embark on risky terrains, living life with audacity is about having the courage to explore uncharted territories, plunge headfirst into the mysterious, trust the unpredictable voyage, and celebrate every twist and turn of life. When we embrace audacity, we propel ourselves past the confines of comfort and into the realm of the extraordinary, much akin to my own journey where I stared life's adversities in the face with a lionhearted spirit and unshakeable resolve.

Stepping out from their protective shells and navigating hazardous routes, turtles symbolize a silent audacity, a testament to their survival that we often fail to acknowledge. To be audacious, in the deepest sense, is to dare to take risks, to dive fearlessly into the unknown, and to harbor faith in the journey, despite the shadows of uncertainty. It's about acknowledging and cherishing both life's triumphs and trials, all while being fully aware of the inevitable hurdles along the path. I became the embodiment of this audacious spirit, confronting life's hitches and glitches head-on, standing tall with unyielding boldness and tenacity.

Much like turtles that, against the odds, boldly tread toward their destination, we can aspire to embody a similar audacious spirit, squaring off against our fears of the unseen and daring to step out of our comfy cocoons. The audacity of a turtle does not lie in swift, thunderous leaps, but rather in the quiet, steadfast courage to keep advancing, one small yet determined step at a time. This has been my journey too, a mirror image of a turtle's audacity — persisting through thick and thin, daring to defy adversities, and staying steadfastly true to the chosen path.

TURTLE INSIGHTS

1. What are some risks you have taken in your life? Reflect on how they have shaped your personality and outlook.

2. Recall a time when you stepped out of your comfort zone. How did the experience impact your emotional state and perspective on life?

3. Where do you see room for more audacity in your life? Could it be in your personal relationships, your career, or your approach to personal growth?

4. How might embracing audacity improve your life? Can it enhance your personal fulfillment or your relationships with others?

5. Do you know someone who embodies audacity? What characteristics make them audacious, and what can you learn from them?

AFFIRMATIONS

- I am brave enough to step into the unknown and pursue my dreams.

- My audacity guides me to live life to its fullest.

- Every challenge I face is an opportunity for growth.

- I am courageous and capable of navigating any challenge.

- My audacity is the spark that ignites my life's most exciting adventures.

CHAPTER FIVE

Back to Reality

While enjoying the lighter moments, having big fun, carried by waves of laughter and levity, I never lost sight of my duties. Like a turtle, I kept my focus steadfast, remembering the shell of responsibilities I carried. I never forgot that I was a woman full of drive, big goals, and many ambitions who understood the gravity of her responsibilities.

In the daily operation of the business, I was dealing with significant issues filled with outside malice and distractions. Each issue was like a strong wave, threatening to knock me off my path, but I kept my focus and maneuvered through. I negotiated with the government to obtain a long-term lease of a building my company managed while fighting with a union determined to dethrone me and shut down my business. I was a turtle swimming against the currents; I had to remain determined and resilient, persistently moving forward.

Being able to multitask, keep a clear head, and fight envy and jealousy while managing hundreds of people's lives and well-being was a tremendous load to bear. It was a weight as solid and significant as the crown of a queen. The devil you know is always better than the devil you don't know. In other words, it's always preferable to contend with a known challenge than an unknown one. I knew my enemy; it was up to the enemy to know who they were fighting—the key to winning lies in the preparation. I understood that failing to prepare meant I was, in essence, preparing for failure. This little Haitian girl had grown to become a force to be reckoned with. Just as a turtle carries its shell, I carried my strength and determination with pride. Through facing trials and surmounting challenges, the wide-eyed black Caribbean girl I once was evolved, molded by the grit of education and experience into a woman standing confidently in her power. Like a diamond pressed and polished by the harsh realities of life, through hard work, sweat, and tears, I was prepared to navigate this harsh and challenging world called America.

I didn't just survive in it—I thrived in it. And I made sure to do so with style and respect for others. I did it with class, dignity, and prestige. I owned and served as the chief executive officer of Washington, D.C.'s only minority-certified, woman-owned nursing home business. I can say with certainty that I was the envy of many. I left a trail of stardust behind me with each step, eliciting wonder and admiration—though not without making some people jealous. Like a turtle, I moved forward at my own pace, unperturbed by the ripples I caused in the pond of my industry. But I knew that I was surrounded by alligators, ready to strike if I showed any sign of weakness.

An enormous alligator was lurking in the shadowy waters—one of these organizing groups' many vice presidents determined to unionize my staff. He was one of my countrymen, a "Haitian man." He was not a member of the Washington, D.C. union crew; however, he was hand-picked by the union to guarantee the unionization of my business. Because he was Haitian, the thinking was that it would be easier for him to penetrate my circle of friends and make personal contact with me.

I had to give him credit; he had employed a few cunning ploys to get into the Haitian community in Washington, D.C., and set up a meeting with me. But all his efforts were in vain, like a chess move in a game I was all too familiar with. His whole endeavor amounted to nothing more than fruitless entrapments. Just like the organizers in Washington, D.C., he soon discovered that I was a fierce woman, an undersea turtle that was difficult to capture. My education and the tenacity of my beliefs served as my armor. My values and expertise served as a shield to keep him out and keep myself safe from his attempts to intrude.

Like a turtle that doesn't harbor ill-will against the currents, I harbored no ill feelings toward this Haitian man. I understood he had a job to do and I, a business to protect at all costs. This Haitian man, I learned, resided in New York City yet was a frequent flyer to Washington, D.C. to meet with the local organizing union members, a handful of my staff, and some of my professional colleagues. It was a chess game, and every move mattered. This gentleman did everything in his power to secure a private meeting with me but all in vain.

I found strength in the turtle, a creature that hides in its shell when faced with danger, not out of fear, but as a strategic defense. One particular incident stands out vividly in my memory. I received a call from a well-known Haitian physician in the diaspora requesting that I join him for lunch with this Haitian union vice president. A pleasant offer, albeit one laced with ulterior motives. I politely refused the invitation by explaining my position regarding union discussions. I subsequently was invited to a reception at the Haitian Embassy. While at the reception, I was escorted to an office by a mutual friend. In the room was the person who invited me to the party, the physician friend who had extended the lunch invitation, and the organizing union vice president who had flown in from New York to attend this reception.

But I had my defenses—my knowledge and my intuition—ready to counteract any incoming strikes. I was prepared to handle this tricky situation. I call this one the perfect trap. It was like being on a stage, under glaring lights, about to deliver a crucial performance. There was small talk for a few minutes until the conversation started to change. Once I realized the purpose of my presence in the room, I rose from my seat, looked at the three men bold in the face, and without any hesitation, I said, "I guess it's time for me to leave. My labor lawyer forbids me to discuss any union issues without him present."

As I delivered my exit line, I could see their eyes widen, their surprise palpable. Like a turtle slipping back into the safety of the water, I swiftly removed myself from a potentially harmful situation. Uttering not another word, I walked out of the room. I closed the door, leaving all three men dumbfounded, probably speaking among themselves, "What the hell just happened here?" Like a badass girl, I walked down the dozen or so steps to the open room on the embassy's first floor, making small talk on my way to the front door, and exited the building.

The union had my picture on both sides of a truck plastered with lies.

Then, they went even lower; they tried to muddy my reputation, attacking me with the lowest of blows.

When all else failed, they were reduced to supernatural maneuvers. Because I was Haitian, they resorted to exploiting my cultural heritage as a tactic to intimidate me. I remained unshaken, my spirit guarded against their mystical antics.

It was early morning, and the night shift staff was exiting the building via the front door. An employee ran back to the building and barged into my office in a frenzy. "Ms. Vivens, you have got to come outside. Come, come!" She motioned with one hand for me to follow her outside the building.

As I stepped outside, a chill ran down my spine, but I held my composure. I drew from an inner strength that told me I could withstand anything. My administrative assistant and I bolted out into the night, like sprinters at the crack of the starter pistol, followed by our security agent. The night staff and a few day-shift employees coming to the building were all on the street, faces frozen in disbelief and astonishment at what was on the opposite side of the road facing the nursing home door. Under a large tree, its branches outstretched like gnarled fingers in the moonlight, was an undeniable voodoo display— tall and short crosses, the flames of lit candles, and white voodoo designs like cryptic graffiti written on the floor. This magic demonstration was meaningless to me. My thought was, "How low can they go?" Was there really a need to go there, and why?

I put into practice the phrase, "When they go low, you go high," meaning that when they resorted to petty and disrespectful tactics, I would respond with dignity and respect. I asked my administrative assistant to call my son, the company president, and ask him to join us outside. I urged the staff to return to the building or to go home as I had my photo taken with my voodoo exhibit, wearing a defiant smile.

The housekeeping staff cleaned the area, like a well-coordinated cleanup crew after a concert, and life at the nursing home continued that day as if this moment—this surreal, eerie moment—never happened.

I never had any ill feelings about the union movement in the building. Organized unions and their success are the best thing that could have happened in America. The origin of the Labor Union dates back to the 1800s. As an owner, I was a good employer, according to most of my staff. I treated them well not because it was demanded by unions, but because it was the right thing to do. In a way, it was like taking the best page from the union's playbook to guide my actions.

Unfortunately for these organizers, the majority of the workers of my business didn't want a union. And I had to do everything in my power to support the wishes of my staff. The organized group manipulated the minds of a very few while the majority begged me not to allow the union to organize them. As the owner, I found myself in a difficult situation. My life was a tightrope walk, delicately balancing the opposing forces while ensuring the delivery of quality care.

I had to protect the business's five-star rating earned from the American Health Care Association.

US News and World Report recognized our company as a quality nursing home. It was essential to the business that families continued to have faith in our staff and care delivery. I was balancing on that thin line, striving to maintain our employees' trust and uphold our public business persona. My duty was to fulfill my role as the leader while ensuring the company's high standing.

There is a time and a place in life for everything. When there is injustice, employer abuse, and unequal pay, a union is the best recourse; however, in my case, I was my employees' biggest advocate when it came to employee rights. As such, they could not fathom what more a union could offer that they were not already getting.

The employees saw no value in paying dues to a union. At a general staff meeting, I recall an employee shouting from the back of the room, his voice echoing with conviction, "We don't need a union; you are our union."

Before obtaining a formal education, I worked in factories in New York City and later as a nanny in a caucasian family's home. Because of how my experiences had shaped me and how my formal education had helped me progress professionally, I felt ready to assume leadership and become their boss.

Before my formal nursing education, I had been a nursing assistant. Because of this work experience, I could associate myself with and understand the life of a nursing assistant. I would often be seen in the employee cafeteria having lunch with the housekeepers, kitchen workers, and laundry staff. In my business attire, I sat among them, sharing laughs and stories over trays of cafeteria food.

I did see myself as one of them, even though I was their leader. I carried my humble beginnings with me, a reminder of the shared experiences that brought us all together. I was no longer in their position only because I had pursued further education. Among them, they saw me as a girl who had grown from their ranks, educated herself, and become an empowered woman who would eventually lead them. I treated those employees with respect and dignity, as though I was still one of them.

The love and respect we had were mutual. I could see it in the way they would willingly work overtime when needed or how they came to me not just with work-related issues, but also with their personal concerns. And I reciprocated, offering them not just a job, but a support system. Some would attend union meetings, but they didn't leave me in the dark. They'd come to my office afterward, recounting exactly what had happened, who had attended, and what was discussed.

I was comforted by the fact that the staff, seeing me as their role model, assured me they would not join the union. In their eyes and mind, they believed, "If she can do it, I can do it too." Today, I am proud to say quite a few little Solanges Vivens in America are following in my footsteps, or maybe even surpassing me. I firmly believe that an educated girl becomes an empowered woman, and an empowered woman can rule the world. This belief has inspired my work and, in its own way, created a ripple effect, one I am proud to have set in motion.

I showed them that how you start your journey doesn't matter. What's truly worthwhile is reaching the finish line (finishing with a bang!) after overcoming challenges, which makes all the sacrifices along the way worth it. I often imparted the wisdom of the turtle to them—emphasizing that it's not about being the fastest, but rather the one who perseveres, who persists until they cross the finish line with a victorious flourish.

Hard work does not kill. (If it did, I would have been dead a long time ago.) Hard work is not something to be feared. If anything, it's a testament to our strength and endurance. The reward of hard work, I taught my staff, is the feeling we get when we look back and smile. Always aim to do the right thing, striving to do it correctly the first time, and be able to look back with a clear conscience, knowing you've done your best. The real prize is not the external recognition but the feeling of accomplishment that swells in your heart when you've done your best.

Turtle Wisdom: Stand Your Ground

When confronted with dangers, a turtle instinctively retreats into its robust shell, a fortified sanctuary that holds steady and does not yield an inch. This reflex is a powerful emblem of resilience, steadfastness, and the fundamental principle of asserting one's position. In this chapter, I channel that emblematic resilience of a turtle, firmly asserting my ground, unflinching in the face of manipulative stratagems. As the turtle retreats into its resilient shell for safety, I too, hold my space, and I hope my narrative inspires you to do the same. I wish for my journey to resonate, emphasizing the potency of resilience, the significance of setting boundaries, and the absolute necessity of holding your ground when challenged.

In life, we are frequently thrown into situations that stretch our patience, test our endurance, and nudge us into uncomfortable corners. These trials may come in various forms; they could be professional hurdles, strains in personal relationships, or just circumstances that challenge our core values. Recognizing our inherent rights, staying true to our values, and learning to defend ourselves is an essential life lesson we all need to grasp. Taking cues from my own experiences and the turtle's symbolic gesture of drawing into its shell, we learn the importance of holding our ground and not allowing anyone or anything to compromise our principles.

TURTLE INSIGHTS

1. Can you recall an instance where you had to assert yourself in a challenging situation? What hurdles did you face, and how did you triumph?

2. What are your uncompromising values and personal boundaries? How do you relay these boundaries to others and ensure they're respected?

3. Have you ever found yourself in a situation where you were unable to assert your position? What lessons did that experience teach you?

4. What strategies can you employ to be more assertive and resolute in defending your personal space and values?

5. In what ways could the turtle's defensive mechanism of retreating into its shell for safety inspire you to be more steadfast and assertive in your life?

AFFIRMATIONS

- I have the strength and resilience to defend my values and boundaries.

- Like the turtle, I am secure within my shell, standing my ground when necessary.

- I respect my own boundaries and demand the same respect from others.

- I am confident in my ability to assert and protect my space.

- Every day, I grow stronger in defending my values, embracing life's challenges with determination and courage.

CHAPTER SIX

Dramas and Triumphs

In the vibrant, ever-changing decade of the early 1990s, I found a transformative book that would become a cornerstone of my journey, *Live Your Dreams*, authored by the passionate and inspiring Les Brown.

Les Brown's powerful, no-holds-barred transparency astounded me when it came to sharing his personal life and experiences with authenticity and openness. As I read, I revisited the rough patches in my own life and dreamed of the day when I, too, could crystallize my experiences into a book—a beacon of hope that might light the way for future generations. An inspirational manual that could spur young minds to carve out their own success stories, just as Mr. Brown's book did for me.

Freshly inspired by *Live Your Dreams*, I learned that while I may not always have control over what life presents to me, I always have a choice in who I become. I traveled with a black-and-white composition notebook, ready to capture my life's pivotal moments. Unfamiliar with the clunky typewriters of the pre-computer age, I found my comfort in the humble pages of composition notebooks, where I began to record my life's narrative across about twenty-two volumes.

I also used six cassette tapes to record my parents as we talked and reminisced.

Their voices continued to resonate in the tapes long after their departure from this world, and I continued to spill my heart into my trusty composition notebooks.

After selling my company nearly thirty years later, I found the time was ripe to take on the task of writing a book. With plenty of free time and no company affairs to manage, I undertook the painstaking process of typing with two fingers on a sleek laptop computer, diligently transferring the information from my composition notebooks and cassette tapes to create a manuscript. Much like a turtle's determined journey toward the ocean, this endeavor spanned a year, from June 2018 to July 2019, as I slowly but surely crafted a manuscript that could be understood by others.

I returned to my house in Barbados with my niece Ingrid, who ended up being an essential part of my writing journey, and we worked nonstop on the manuscript for two relentless weeks.

She patiently combed through my transcriptions, refining and correcting as needed. My second editor was my son Kevin. He held the mantle of editor-in-chief in our company, and I wanted him to feel comfortable with the content. It was not only my history; it was his, and his dad's as well. It was important to me that he be comfortable with all this information put out in the universe.

The following phase was to identify a professional editor who could polish my manuscript and shape it into a publishable book. As luck would have it, I was introduced to a Haitian woman who seemed to be the answer to my prayers. M.J. Fievre is a celebrated writer and the proprietor of a flourishing arts and letters company.

She was able to connect deeply with my narrative, given our shared Haitian heritage. She proposed tweaking the book's title from *A Girl Named Solanges with an S* to *Girls Can Move Mountains*, a suggestion I was quick to agree with.

Together, we invested immense effort to transform my long-cherished dream of publishing my memoir into a tangible reality by crafting a polished, print-ready manuscript. Like a turtle steadfast in its course, regardless of the obstacles, M.J. proved knowledgeable, creative, and enjoyable to collaborate with. She also emerged as a trusted ally and, over time, a cherished friend. Her invaluable input played a significant role in integrating my passion for turtles into the narrative. Holding the finished product in my hands filled me with a sense of exhilaration and immense pride.

In the slow but unwavering pace of a turtle, the journey from reading *Live Your Dreams* to mustering the courage to publish my own life's chronicles spanned over two decades. Much like Les Brown's memoir, my book traces my expedition from the harsh confines of poverty to the heady heights of wealth. I was braced and eager to advance further into the process. M.J. ingeniously revised the book's title to reflect my life story after reading it.

The manuscript contains many accounts of challenges I had to overcome, and M.J. was able to distill this struggle into an apt book title. Her creative prowess shone through in this task. As I navigated the winding paths of life, I encountered increasingly towering, jagged, and steep mountains at every turn. However, I was always able to find a way to navigate each mountain, recovering from each trial and mustering the strength to face the next one.

It was in these moments of immense success and painful setbacks, I felt akin to a turtle, pushing through the sands of life with a resilient shell of determination and hope.

Publishing a book, I discovered, is like a turtle's long journey to the ocean—full of unexpected turns and obstacles. At this juncture, I was ready to embark on the next phase, which involved securing a publishing house that would accept my manuscript. To translate this into reality, I had to secure a contract to get the book published. As an experienced executive, I was acutely aware that the failure to prepare was akin to preparing to fail. I knew I had to arm myself with a deep understanding of the publishing process to taste success.

While attending a glitzy black-tie event hosted by Leadership of Greater Washington, I made a successful bid at a silent auction for an opportunity to share a meal with the celebrated Kitty Kelly. Ms. Kelly has earned acclaim for her detailed biographies of high-profile personalities such as Jacqueline Kennedy Onassis, Elizabeth Taylor, Frank Sinatra, among others. Just as a turtle might find an unexpected current in the sea, I found myself swept into a new and exciting world. However, with resources on my side this time, I saw this auction not as a luxury but a necessary investment. Money, in my view, is not a source of pleasure but a tool we wield to fulfill our needs. I was one of the lucky ones who had the opportunity to take advantage of this silent auction offer.

By winning this bid, I had the chance of a lifetime to interact with a famous biographical author. I obtained first-hand knowledge about the ins and outs of the publishing world, a key that could unlock many doors. My mind was abuzz with anticipation, conjuring up all manner of visions, up to and including obtaining a publisher's recommendation letter from Ms. Kelly herself. My mind was a whirlwind of excitement and anticipation, right up until the moment I met her. In my opinion, it was money well spent, and then some.

However, I can't help but reflect on the disparity between privilege and need, on the haves and the have-nots, and the opportunities that slip away when we lack resources or knowledge. I'm reminded of the times when the world of black-tie galas was a distant, alien landscape, when the thought of penning a book seemed as plausible as flying to the moon. Alas, not everyone can seize the opportunities life tosses our way, simply because we haven't learned the ropes or we lack the means to participate. Books like Les Brown's *Live Your Dreams*, my own book, *Girls Can Move*

Mountains, and many others are written with a singular purpose in mind: to show those less fortunate how to bridge the gap between the have-nots and the haves; all it takes is a little self-trust. Take a long, hard look at the girl staring back at you in the mirror. Make her a promise that you'll do right by her, that you'll be her safety net, her source of unconditional love, and that you'd even lay down your life for her.

At the prestigious Georgetown Inn in Washington, D.C., I savored an unforgettable, insightful lunch with Ms. Kelly. For a moment, I believed I had died and gone to heaven. Here was this Haitian girl, once again rubbing shoulders with the high society, scaling mountains of prestige in the presence of a celebrated author. Ms. Kelly was the embodiment of grace and dignity, treating me as a fellow author with respect and camaraderie. Her words were interwoven with humor and a warmth that radiated intelligence and infectious charisma.

In her company was Linda Cashden, a fellow novelist and editor, who graciously offered to peruse the first three chapters of my book. Although my bid was for lunch with Ms. Kelly, and we didn't maintain contact afterward, Linda stayed in touch. It felt as if Ms. Kelly had subtly passed the torch to Linda, entrusting her with the task of holding my hand through the process.

She proved to be an invaluable resource, providing insightful advice and guidance. I would send her book proposals intended for various publishing houses for a final review before mailing them off. Her feedback was concise, constructive, and always on point.

However, I must admit, it was disheartening to receive less enthusiastic responses than I expected for my proposals. Some publishers didn't even extend the courtesy of a response, while others sent polite but nonetheless disheartening rejection emails. A few requested the first fifty pages of the manuscript before ultimately declining due to an overwhelming workload. Another publisher expressed interest in my book but mentioned a potential wait of two years. They asked if I could be patient for that long. I had complete faith in my story and in the quality and relevance of my writing. These rejections were a bitter pill to swallow.

Despite these setbacks, my resolve to find a traditional publisher remained firm. I considered the option of self-publishing, but I quickly set aside these thoughts as I desired the wider reach and professional touch a traditional publisher could provide. To add insult to injury, speaking engagements that I had lined up started falling through. A speaking engagement at a Nurses Week celebration for a significant hospital chain that I was slated to appear at was abruptly canceled for reasons that were never disclosed.

By this point, the string of rejections had taken its toll. My frustration had reached a boiling point, which I vented to a close male friend. He suggested I run a search for my name on social media. I had never dabbled in social media, viewing it as a frivolous pastime best suited to the youth or those with too much time on their hands. With my hands full managing a large company, I was blissfully ignorant of the power and influence that social media wielded.

My foray into the world of social media opened my eyes to a side of public perception I had not previously considered. I was stunned and incensed by what I was reading about myself. It was beyond comprehension that someone could stoop so low as to slander me on a public platform. In our company, we had a workforce of about eight hundred employees. I had deliberately stayed away from social media to avoid the added expectations from others, chiefly my staff.

And now, much to my chagrin, I found myself thrust into yet another battleground. My online reputation had been tarnished, which suddenly explained the slew of rejections and cancellations. I was now faced with a daunting new challenge: How to defend myself against such damaging public slander? The anger welled up inside me, leaving a bitter taste. I was advised to hire a reputation management company, which meant I was staring down the barrel of yet another costly legal skirmish—the who, what, when, and where began to flash before my eyes.

Overwhelmed with anger, I realized I needed professional help to navigate this. But where was I to start? How does one go about locating a reputation management coach? Who exactly delves into this peculiar line of work? What might be the cost of such an unusual service? Questions swirled around me like a flock of birds in a stormy sky. I felt like a fish out of water, completely out of my element and rather lost. To fight the ghosts of past conflicts that had unexpectedly re-emerged in my present, I realized I had no choice but to step up and morph into a formidable force, a badass retiree to match up to the notorious bad boys I was dealing with.

And much like a lone ship on stormy seas, even in the face of adversity, I pressed on, propelled by an innate sense of survival and an unwavering resolve. My good friend Cyrel, with a reassuring firmness in his voice, asked me to sit tight and allow him a few weeks to probe into my vexing situation. As I found myself embroiled in this unexpected predicament, I patiently waited in prayer. Despite the whirlwind of confusion and the prickling irritation, one emotion I refused to succumb to was fear. I recognized fear for what it was, a crippling adversary that could hinder any hope for a positive resolution.

Having always been a person anchored in faith, I held onto the belief that God would guide me through this storm, for He was, after all, the fountainhead of all solutions. As I delved deeper into the murky waters of my predicament, I unearthed a startling revelation: the negative social media posts, which were causing such a ruckus now, had been silently lurking around since my union involvement years ago. At that time, these posts had remained benign, largely because social media was not the go-to platform for anyone outside of my professional circle in the long-term care sector.

The insidious slanders and half-truths that had been flung about on social media would have been largely dismissed by those in my close professional circle, who knew my work ethic and integrity. They would have easily recognized it for what it was—nothing more than smoke and mirrors, a byproduct of union politics. However, with the advent of my book, a new and wider audience had begun to show interest in me. This audience included hospital administrators, CEOs, and publishing company consultants.

In the brave new world of the 21st century, social media has emerged as the all-seeing, all-knowing oracle, the first point of reference to know someone. Within this context, my reputation had been marred, stained with untruths, causing potential collaborators to take a step back. Recognizing the gravity of the situation, I took decisive action and sought out the help of an organization specializing in reputation management. They helped scrub away the defamatory lies, the union misrepresentations, and other harmful information, albeit at a substantial cost.

Emboldened and with a renewed sense of hope, I sent my proposal to a renowned publishing house, and, much to my delight, it was greenlit for publication within a few days of submission. The realization of why my manuscript had previously been overlooked or rejected hit me like an unexpected wave—a genuine moment of clarity. As the old saying goes, "Sticks and stones may break my bones, but words shall never harm me."

With the feeling of accomplishment came a sense of relief. I moved ahead, embarking on my journey as a published author, carrying with me the silent fortitude of the turtle.

Turtle Wisdom: Patience Brings Reward

Much like the delicate yet unwavering journey of a turtle, life too unfolds in its own rhythm, demanding patience and tenacity to bear its fruits. In the silent depth of the ocean, a turtle mother lays her eggs, giving way to a cycle of life, a testament to her perseverance and trust in the passage of time. Similarly, the journey of publishing this memoir was a marathon, not a sprint, speckled with rejections and stumbling blocks. Yet, at the end of this enduring path, the rewards unfolded, proving to be more enriching than I could have ever imagined.

When we apply this turtle insight to the canvas of our own lives, we find that some goals, aspirations, and interpersonal connections frequently develop gradually and require time to mature. Just as the turtle eggs nestle quietly in the sand until nature decides they're ready to break free, we too are called upon to practice patience and trust in the organic flow of life. This waiting phase can be a roller coaster of feelings—a mixture of doubt, rejection, and uncertainty. However, this memoir shows us that when we persevere, the rewards we receive in the end are frequently more than we could have imagined.

TURTLE INSIGHTS

1. Reflect on a facet of your life that currently demands your patience. How are you responding to this call?

2. Rejections and disappointments are a part of life's journey. How do you cope with these setbacks? What coping mechanisms do you employ?

3. Can you look back and identify any invaluable lessons you've gathered from periods of patient waiting?

4. Think of a moment when your patience finally bore fruit. What was it like? How did you feel?

5. In what ways can you channel the wisdom of the turtle—that patience culminates in reward—in your present circumstances?

AFFIRMATIONS

- I have the patience and perseverance to reach my goals.

- My journey is not defined by the rejections I encounter, but by my resolve to keep going.

- I trust in the timing of my life, understanding that every stage has its purpose.

- I embrace the waiting periods in my life as opportunities for growth and reflection.

- Like a turtle, I am relentless in my pursuit, knowing that patience will bring my reward.

CHAPTER SEVEN

The Good, the Bad, and the Ugly

Remaining relevant and active, both mentally and physically, is essential as we age. Women are increasingly working into their mid-seventies and living a very active life, embracing the age with a gusto that paints a vibrant image of longevity. As a young adult, I pledged to emulate the gutsy attitude, stamina, and tenacity of the female role models I admired—their spirits guiding me like a torch lighting a path through the dark. While trying to figure out my path in the seventies, I recalled Shirley Chisholm, an American woman born to Caribbean parents. This trailblazer, who cut her own way through the thickest of social norms, was the first black woman to dare run for president of the United States of America. She was asked in an interview how she would like to be remembered. She answered, "You don't make progress by standing on the sideline, whimpering and complaining. You make progress by implementing ideas." It was clear that she wanted to be remembered as a progressive.

At a decision point, I realized that education was everything. You need to be educated to become powerful—to become somebody in this world. Understanding that power lies in education and that knowledge is the backbone of this power, I took to heart the slogan: "An educated consumer is our best customer." In my life, I prioritized education as a means of harnessing power. With every book read, every lecture attended, and every degree earned, I saw doors opening, opportunities arising, and my influence in my field growing. Like the fierce ray of a lighthouse guiding ships through the murky darkness, education illuminated my path. I educated myself to the highest degree possible in the health care field.

As I continued to grow in business and better understand the value of wisdom, I looked up to women who made a difference regardless of their age or the industry in which they practiced. As I write this chapter, Nancy Pelosi, the vivacious eighty-two-year-old speaker of the house, and our sassy vocalists, Tina Turner, Cher, and others, have me spellbound. Their voices echo through time, their vibrant spirits lighting up the stage of life. I adopted this attitude: "If they can do it, so can I." Their determined spirits echoed the perseverance of a turtle, pushing forward against any current. I sold my business and embarked on a new journey. I became an author of inspirational books and an international public speaker on women's empowerment.

The baby boomers have redefined retirement, embracing life's opportunities regardless of age. Women at any age have become increasingly educated, more and more productive regardless of age, and are playing just as hard as they have worked. We've redefined age to be nothing more than a number, a simple digit that does not dictate our passion or limit our dreams. Just as we've broken barriers in our careers, we've rewritten the rules in the game of love, casting aside the age-old playbook. It became fashionable for older women to be intimately involved with men who were several years their junior. Like lionesses owning the savannah, these women courageously embraced the unknown with audacity and allure. Throughout their lives, the baby boomer generation has challenged many social norms—introducing flexible work hours, popularizing the idea of a second career, and embracing an active lifestyle beyond retirement—and thus carved out a distinct identity.

Around 1999, the term cougar was developed in Canada to define middle-aged women in a romantic relationship with a younger man. This phenomenon has advantages but also comes with how one moves forward in an age disparity relationship. Clifford was a few years younger, yet I was much younger in spirit, always ready to go and full of energy. When I transitioned from responsibility for others to a life of fun and traveling the world, he made it clear that he would not only work for many more years, he intended to retain an office at the law firm even after his retirement to spend quiet time writing a book.

Despite our shared history, we eventually found our visions for the future at odds. Our anticipated future turned into a battleground, with desires clashing in heated debates, leaving no resolution in sight. This was no mere skirmish in the realm of love, but rather a fierce battle of wills and wants. I wanted us to sell our houses and move together into a condominium away from the responsibilities of maintaining a property. He wanted me to move in with him at his house. During one of those conversations about our future together, he made a disastrous move when he said, "I am the man; you should move in with me." That statement's insinuation was the final straw for me; it was never going to work. He returned the key to my front door—we called it quits on our amazing thirteen-year romance. Still, we continue to care for each other as friends. He provided legal services to me personally and to the business until it was sold.

Once the *Girls Can Move Mountains* manuscript was in the hands of a publishing company, I found myself with an abundance of free time. It was a time ripe for mischief, for diving headfirst into new projects, or simply basking in the quiet moments. A sea of possibilities lay before me, as endless and inviting as the horizon on a summer's day. Much like a turtle with an open ocean before her, my mind was racing for the next big endeavor. I had to develop a new strategy since Clifford was no longer my traveling companion. It was an intimidating yet exhilarating prospect. If there was one aspect of our relationship that I mourned immediately after the breakup, it was all the trips I would miss by not having him as my traveling companion. However, as a rule, I never allowed fear to halt me in my tracks because it would paralyze me. I convinced myself there are countless paths winding toward the same destination—the freedom and fulfillment I yearned for could be attained through various means, not just through a romantic relationship. I then asked Solanges, "If not Clifford, then who?" I turned my attention back to me, the girl in the mirror. I was unsure of my next move, yet I was confident I did not possess the dormant procrastinator type of personality. I was ready to spread my wings and catch the wind, ready to take flight into the boundless sky of opportunities.

Like a turtle embracing the currents, changing course with the tides, I aspired to stay engaged and dynamic, both socially and personally. I sold my business, then sold my beautiful huge house in Rock Creek Park in D.C. With the fruits of this transition, I found myself the owner of a luxurious, sunlight-drenched four-bedroom condominium in the bustling heart of Bethesda, Maryland, and a captivating little mansion perched by a serene lake in sun-kissed Florida. While the newfound freedom was exhilarating, it was not without its challenges. With no man, no child, no work, I was worry-free to do whatever I wanted, whenever I wanted, and go where I pleased with whomever I desired. But with that freedom also came moments of introspection, loneliness, and readjustments. Nevertheless, I saw it as a path to a new chapter of self-discovery and growth. I reached out to family and friends. I had the time and means and was out to have big clean fun.

Basking in the glow of my unfettered freedom, I found myself on the hunt for new adventures. One day, I happened to overhear two mutual friends, Grace and Earline, excitedly discussing a trip they were planning to Johannesburg, South Africa. Their talk of wine tastings and safari expeditions roused my latent desire. Their shouts carried a contagious excitement that made me want to rush in and join them. I jumped right into their conversation with all the energy of a happy child, asking excitedly if I might participate. Grace smiled and prodded Earline to turn to look at me. They enthusiastically welcomed my interruption and invited me to come along on their next trip to Johannesburg, South Africa, where they would be spending Christmas and New Year's Eve.

Oh, what a treat that was! Our little group consisted of two couples, one with two lively teenage daughters, and then there was me—the lone adventurer, relishing my freedom. But I was unfazed by this unusual combination. As a comforting presence and a familiar safety net, my friends were there, but I insisted on having my own agenda. With or without a companion, I wanted to be open to discovery and take advantage of everything Johannesburg had to offer.

As the days went by, my fellow travelers found happiness at our hotel's bar, where they laughed and told stories far into the night. I discovered that, despite missing their companionship, I was more drawn to the peaceful stillness of my room and the prospect of early morning activities. I deliberately chose to go to bed early every night in order to enjoy the early mornings. I would awaken with the dawn, eager to embrace the adventures that were ahead of me. I began my excursions with an exhilarating minivan safari tour, which gave me a close-up look at magnificent animals in their unique natural habitat.

Then I spent a day hopping from one winery to another, savoring the rich and complex flavors of South African wine.

The sweet, mellow taste of the wine seemed to mirror the welcoming warmth of the people I met. I spent an entire day in Mandela Square, sightseeing.

By the time I got off the bus, I had become friends with practically everyone, and our days were spent laughing and telling interesting stories to each other. I was going to soak in every bit of this South African experience.

Our group ventured into Soweto, a Johannesburg township renowned for its critical role in South Africa's fight against apartheid. However, due to the sensitive nature of the area, officers told us we could only visit Soweto if invited by a resident. Back at the hotel, we were given the unique opportunity to be the guests of a woman who lived in Soweto—the warm and friendly bartender my travel companions had befriended.

After leaving the hotel, we walked a few blocks ahead of our host to protect her employment and prevent unwanted attention. This cloak-and-dagger activity was quite exhilarating because of the thrill of doing something a little unlawful. In Soweto, we saw glimmers of progress with newly constructed, modern homes dotting the landscape, their indoor toilets a testament to improving living conditions for the community.

Our adventures took us to the stunning Tabletop Mountain, where we journeyed via cable cars and encountered wildlife as majestic as the journey itself.

Particularly, the serenity and steadfastness of turtles that we spotted basking on the shores or swimming in the distance had a recurring soothing presence, reminding us of the endurance of life's journeys.

Our trip took a surprising turn when we visited Robben Island, where Nelson Mandela was imprisoned. There, while sharing light-hearted banter with the ship's captain, I was surprised to see Jean Bertrand Aristide, the former president of Haiti, and his wife. We spent the rest of our journey reminiscing about the motherland. This unexpected reunion, combined with our visit to Desmond Tutu's church, added a rich layer of personal connection and historical reverence to our trip, truly making it an unforgettable experience.

My butterfly friend Ana and I decided to take our wanderlust to India, joining a luxury travel group operated by Abercrombie & Kent.

One of the many highlights of this trip was our day spent at the breathtaking Taj Mahal, an ivory-white marble monument that stood proudly against the azure Indian sky, its stunning architecture a testament to an age-old love story. This was a moment I had dreamed of, and standing before the Taj Mahal, I felt a wave of awe and admiration wash over me.

We journeyed across India, traveling by plane and ship to various cities. We explored both the ancient and modern facets of Delhi. In Udaipur, we had the privilege of staying at the Udaipur Taj Lake Palace Hotel, once the summer residence of the Mewar Royal Family until its conversion into a hotel in 1963. During our stay, the sole means of transportation to and from the shores was by tender.

The next leg of our journey in India was both exhilarating and daring. From India, Ana and I flew to Nepal, where our adventures continued. With a defiant spirit, I boarded a two-seater helicopter, ready to soar toward the towering peak of Mount Everest.

As I stepped into the helicopter, a rush of adrenaline coursed through my veins, satisfying my thirst for adventure. As we ascended, the world below seemed to shrink, and my fear was replaced with pure joy. As I faced Everest head-on, I realized that this was truly a once-in-a-lifetime experience, a memory etched into my very being. The pilot surprised me with an unexpected detour before returning to the airport. He landed on a mountain near Mount Everest, where we enjoyed a delightful breakfast with the majestic Everest as our backdrop.

Having worked in long-term care for over forty years, I had a keen awareness of how age could potentially limit my travel. Yet, I was determined to seize every opportunity for adventure while I could. I knew that in the future, I would cherish the ability to look back at these incredible and enjoyable experiences through videos and photos. Understanding that my days of world travel would eventually come to an end, I made a promise to myself to savor each moment. Surrounded by the sights and sounds of wildlife in their natural habitats, I spent a blissful afternoon riding an elephant.

This was a joyous experience that brought me immense peace and contentment.

Back home, I continued to nurture my friendship with Christina, my classmate from the Leadership of Greater Washington program, a prestigious course for current and emerging leaders in the region. We formed a close-knit group of about six women, aptly named the "Divas," and found common ground in our shared experiences as busy executives. We made it a point to meet once a month for a fun-filled dinner at a member's house, creating a support system where we could lean on each other. Christina and I, especially, found our personalities to be strikingly similar, and our public interactions often led to hilarious bouts of confusion due to our shared nickname, "Chica." But these light-hearted mix-ups only added to the charm of our camaraderie and lifted our spirits.

At a dinner hosted at my home, the Divas basked in the warm, flickering glow of the evening, our laughter resounding through the halls. As we chilled out in the living room, chatting and sipping champagne, each one of us was wrapped comfortably in the luxury of the tufted armchairs, enjoying the tickling sensation of the carbonation dancing on our tongues. Christina reached out to a copy of Abercrombie and Kent's Luxury Small Group Journeys magazine on my coffee table. This magazine, its glossy pages filled with far-flung destinations, opened a window to exhilarating escapades, a tantalizing ticket to travel. "Why don't we go to Vietnam?" Christina asked. Without any hesitation, I yelled, "Count me in!"

Christina and I, brimming with excitement, immediately set a time to indulge in the thrilling process of trip planning. In just a few months, we were on an airplane heading to Vietnam as anticipation tingled in our veins, our hearts pounding in the rhythm of adventure. After a very long flight, we eventually arrived at the hotel. We immediately went to the spa for a two-hour massage and steam. We could barely eat dinner before dozing off under the embrace of silky sheets, letting the weariness of travel melt into sweet dreams.

Day after day, we journeyed from one captivating site to another, drinking in the rich history and vibrant culture around us. In Ho Chi Minh City, once known as Saigon during the Vietnam War, I crammed myself into a small underground passage, big enough to fit my body with both arms extended in the air.

I slowly and finally reached the ground after descending a series of steps. Incredibly, the tunnel network stretched for approximately one hundred and twenty-eight kilometers, deep and wide enough to include a hospital and all the amenities necessary for an underground life during wartime. This amazing display of human resourcefulness and tenacity highlighted the intricate past we were studying. I was awakened to the drama and pain of war by this specific encounter.

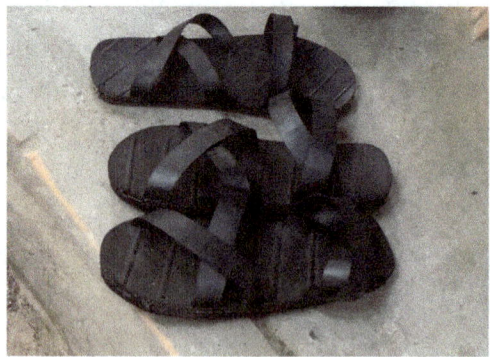

Vietnamese soldiers were never apprehended when U.S. soldiers were pursuing them on foot because their tracks were pointing in the opposite direction. It is mind-boggling how the Vietnamese designed shoes with reverse shoe prints and created the underground concealment concept of war. My trip to Vietnam was most memorable and educational because of this excursion.

During the tour, we went to the earliest university built in the country, where a stunning cement wall had giant, lifelike turtles sculpted on it as a symbol of wisdom and tenacity to encourage the students. I was reminded once more of the great wisdom contained in the lowly shape of the turtle. I picked the turtle as my adopted animal for my book *Girls Can Move Mountains*. Enlightenment permeated the air as I took in all the symbolism around me and the silent tales of courage and wisdom carved into the stone. Turtles cannot travel backward and must stretch their necks out to move ahead, which is why they are my favorite animal and the mascot of this university. It is no secret that I like to compare my personal life to that of the turtle, so I was in turtle heaven once more. During our time in Vietnam, I had some of the most incredibly amazing travel experiences of my life. After leaving Vietnam, we traveled to Cambodia and enjoyed its extensive history. After that, we took a plane to Thailand, where we explored its thriving cities and tranquil temples before returning to the United States.

Friend requests for trip companions were coming in, and I rarely declined them. From Barbados, my girlfriend Ann called to invite me to join her and two of her close friends, Ann and Beverly, on a European cruise to celebrate her 70th birthday.

I love to travel. I was always ready to go on another trip. I couldn't care less where we were going; all I wanted to know was the departure and return dates for my availability. We took a Mediterranean cruise, making stops in Barcelona and Naples, before finally reaching our destination in Madrid, Spain. Despite the drama of being in a severe thunderstorm at sea and having only recently met Ann's friends, I had the loveliest time. As the mighty ocean roared around us, its icy fingers clawing at our vessel, we stood firm in the face of the storm, embracing the adrenaline rush of a thrill-packed adventure.

While I was on the Barcelona trip, I received a call from my sister/friend Gloria informing me of a brand-new Caribbean cruise ship that was going to be christened by Oprah Winfrey! Gloria was so excited while telling me the tickets were very limited. "I want to go," she said, "and I want YOU to go with me!" Our tickets were purchased and off we went on a cruise with OPRAH! The ship was huge, the events were great, the food was wonderful, and Gail King very graciously took pictures with hundreds of women. Throughout the journey, we saw Oprah once, live on stage in a beautiful theatre on the ship. It was an amazing experience to be entertained by the very charming and eloquent Oprah Winfrey. We had big fun in great company.

Whenever I returned from a trip with friends, I often relived the experience with my sisters. Either we visited the same destinations, or I took them to a location of their choice. I frequently organized these excursions for up to five sisters at a time and sometimes would include my brothers as well.

Together, we journeyed on horseback through Punta Cana, delved into the lush tropics of Hawaii, marveled at the engineering feats of the Panama Canal, and lounged on the sun-drenched beaches of Saint Lucia—where we indulged in a mud bath—among other captivating destinations.

ST. LUCIA

PUNTA CANA

ALTUN HA, IN BELIZE

HAWAII

My sister Antonine and I ventured to Cuba on a thrilling, women-only clandestine expedition.

I then went to the Island of Guadeloupe for a real crazy time with my cousins Christine and Florence.

LOURDES

Each trip was like flipping a page in an enchanting book, revealing an array of vibrant cultures, tantalizing cuisines, and landscapes painted with the vibrant hues of nature's palette.

I traveled to Bourges, France, this time with my niece Lynda for the Pentecost Monday Procession at Saint Solange village. I learned of the annual procession when I discovered Saint Solange, with whom I shared the same name. Every year, I have made it a point to visit this small community where I have earned the nickname "American Lady," bringing a different member of my family or acquaintance along. To my knowledge, aside from Father Jean Mari—the first African Nigerian priest appointed to the village—I am the only other regular black visitor to the area.

Many Portuguese people have long embraced Saint Solange as their patron saint. Every year on Pentecost Monday, they come to take part in the procession and perform in a concert that evening. It is an all-day celebration that includes food, drink, music, and lots of dancing till dusk on the chapel grounds. The vibrant ambiance of the festival is filled with a kaleidoscope of sights and sounds, including the rich melody of traditional Portuguese music and the enticing perfume of grilled sardines and other delicacies.

Not far from the festivities stands a picturesque chapel, built in the 1800s as a testament to the village's enduring faith. It is maintained by the villagers who struggle to keep it as best as they can. So far, I have replaced the windows that desperately needed repair; I have just had the exterior painted and replaced the gutters. My last project is installing a new roof as the current leaks and stains the inside walls. Every hammer strike, every brush stroke, was an expression of my love and commitment to preserving this charming symbol of faith, leaving my imprint its centuries-old legacy.

The year 2024 will mark the one-hundred-and-fiftieth anniversary of the annual Pentecost Monday celebration. A bigger processional celebration is in the plan. I pray that I am healthy enough to make this trip to Saint Solange Village one last time to celebrate our shared name and birthday.

I had traveled with my sisters and individual nieces for several years, but I had never traveled with my nieces as a group. I was about to turn seventy-three years old. I decided to celebrate by asking my nieces to join me on a trip to Antigua if they could free themselves from their day-to-day life activities as working women for a well-deserved week of rest and bonding and empowerment with their very own Ma Tante Soso.

I had been traveling locally and internationally and realized that this group of young women in my own family could benefit from a health, wellness, and mentoring excursion. Thus, after sending out an enticing email invitation, I received a resounding yes from all twelve ladies invited.

The email stated, "You have been invited to travel to Antigua with me for my seventy-third birthday celebration of life for a week of family team building, women's leadership training, thought-provoking and growth-producing week while reconnecting with each other.

This journey turned out to be a wonderful experience not only for my nieces but for me as well. Together, we had the opportunity to decompress from our lives as working women, wives, and moms. Many cousins had not seen or been with each other for years, so it was a sweet gathering. I had an opportunity to really get to know those young women since the distance between us was now closed.

Having my own suite allowed me to prepare for our daily empowerment sessions. I turned my living room into a meeting room and grouped thirteen chairs into a circle for us to talk about our current lives and forecast future goals after we returned from breakfast every morning. From there, we ventured out for the day, contemplating our educational meeting, enjoying the island sun, and spending quality time with each other.

On our first day, we began by taking a group picture on the steps of our hotel, followed by an evening dinner on the beach. We started my birthday celebration with a sunrise walk on the beach, where we welcomed the new day of my seventy-third year. We breakfasted together, and even on my birthday, we had a session on life in general. We partied on a mountaintop, visited a neighboring beach resort, went sightseeing via a boat ride, and toured the island. We danced in the moonlight together and were treated to a spa massage.

My nieces continuously express that the most priceless gift they garnered from the Antigua trip was the mentoring sessions that inspired and motivated them to go back to their lives with renewed vigor, vitality, and aspirations to move forward professionally and share those aspirations with their families. At every family gathering, at least one of the nieces will recap how they've all grown, changed, and moved on for the better and thank me daily for being such a beacon of light, helping them see the path they should follow, which warms my heart.

The day before we returned to the United States from Antigua, I woke up blind. I shockingly could not see enough to read or recognize faces. I could put on my clothes and walk about with extreme care. I was terrified but decided not to share this with my nieces so I would not spoil this precious holiday. I spent the whole day faking it.

I had planned a farewell dinner at a particular restaurant that was highly recommended and one not to be missed. The dinner was à la carte, and I could not read the menu. I jokingly turned to one of my youngest nieces, Dominique, and said matter-of-factly, "Do you know why we sent you guys to school?" Answering my own question, I replied, "So that you can read to us when we can no longer read for ourselves."

Dominique stated, "Oh yeah, right."

"Go ahead, I'm listening." Dominique read the menu, and when she named an item on the menu that I wanted, I would say, "That sounds good; I want that, and I want you to remember because I would like for you to order for me."

My nieces and I thoroughly enjoyed our last meal in Antigua.

After a lovely breakfast, we departed for the airport the following morning. When we arrived, I realized I could no longer oversee the group as I did when we traveled to the island. I was not able to read any of the signs. All thirteen of us were assembled at the airport with lots of suitcases, trying to figure out our next move, so I spontaneously appointed Marggy to lead our group. She was perfect for the position, immediately becoming our tour guide and escorting us all the way back to my house.

Before we all dissipated, I told them that I woke up blind the day before, which was why I delegated to them all the functions that required reading. In shock, they thanked me for the beautiful trip but left disheartened that such a harsh turn of events had transpired for me.

I had called my sister Antonine from Antigua, who had secured an eye doctor's appointment for me in Florida for the afternoon of our return. The doctor, after some extensive examinations, believed that I had an acute case of Macular Degeneration, and he referred me to a Retina Specialist. He said most likely, the specialist would give me an injection in each eye. I returned to the house and called my eye doctor at Kaiser. Who advised me to come back to Washington, D.C. immediately to be seen by him since he had all my records, and I did. Dominique lives in Maryland and was returning home the next day, so I immediately booked a seat on her flight, and she guided me home. The following day, I was at Kaiser Permanente for care.

I was one of the lucky ones who had macular edema and, with treatment, prevented permanent vision loss. I regained full sight in both eyes. I was fortunate to have gone through this episode while I was in the company of my nieces; however, since this frightening overseas experience, I no longer travel alone.

I fulfilled my deep ambition of exploring the world with the help of my family and friends, who supported my passion for travel. I have shared some of those lovely moments to encourage my readers never to allow age to stop them in their tracks. I remember traveling to Israel with my sisters Antonine and Mirlene, along with my best sister-friend Gloria. Despite all the fears and warnings instilled in us about the dangers of the region, we ventured forth. As we traversed the ancient cobblestone streets of Jerusalem, or waded in the salty buoyancy of the Dead Sea, each moment was a testament to the beauty of exploration and companionship.

However, as wonderful as travel can be, it's important to remember that there's never a guaranteed right time to travel, simply because we can't control Mother Nature. Whether it's an earthquake, a hurricane at sea, an unexpected fire, or political unrest, unpredictable events can happen while on vacation. Everyday activities like driving a car to work or even crossing a street can also pose risks.

I have created memories permanently etched in my brain by not allowing fear or naysayers to stop me from reaching my goals. Life is meant to be lived; just live it with no regrets. You are doing yourself a disservice if you fail to "Live Your Dream." Every sunrise is an opportunity, a call to seize the day, to embark on a new adventure, adding vibrant strokes and limitless possibilities to life. So dance, explore, laugh and love, for life is a canvas waiting for you to paint your story.

Turtle Wisdom: Self-Discovery is a Continuous Process

Consider the baby turtle, freshly hatched and standing on the precipice of the vast ocean. There are no maps, no written instructions, only their primal instincts guiding them toward their destination. This chapter echoes the arduous yet enlightening journey of the baby turtle. Self-discovery isn't an isolated event confined to a single moment but rather a winding path of introspection and growth that spans a lifetime. In this chapter, I embark on my own transformative journey, venturing into uncharted territories of passion and experiences, persistently striving to understand the deepest layers of my being. Just like the baby turtle, who, instead of being daunted by the boundless ocean, wholeheartedly plunges into its expansive depths, I too have made a pact to view my voyage as an endless saga of adventure, brimming with opportunities to evolve and flourish.

Life is notorious for deviating from our meticulously drafted plans, confronting us with unexpected changes and formidable challenges. Yet within the heart of every change, every challenge, resides a chance for self-discovery and reinvention. Time holds no dominion over the commencement of a new chapter, the exploration of unvisited interests, or the unraveling of concealed facets of your persona. Like the turtle, equipped with intuitive wisdom and innate strength for its journey, you too are armed with everything you need to navigate your unique path.

TURTLE INSIGHTS

1. Reflect upon a time when a monumental change rocked your world. How did you adapt and overcome, and what did it reveal about your inherent strength?

2. Are there dormant passions or unexplored interests within you waiting to be unearthed? What barriers are preventing you from pursuing them?

3. What is your interpretation of "self-discovery"? How has your perception of yourself evolved over the years?

4. Contemplate a recent hurdle you managed to overcome. In what ways did it influence your self-perception?

5. Are you welcoming the ongoing journey of self-discovery with open arms, or are you hindering it with resistance? Why is that?

AFFIRMATIONS:

- I am on a continuous journey of self-discovery and self-growth.
- I am open and receptive to new experiences and knowledge.

- I am flexible and adaptable, able to navigate through change and challenges with resilience and grace.

- I have the courage to step out of my comfort zone and explore new aspects of myself.

- I honor and appreciate my journey, knowing that every step brings me closer to my true self.

CHAPTER EIGHT

Work Hard and Play Harder

Because of our inherent warrior spirit, woven into the very fabric of our being, women are effective leaders and triumphant victors. From enduring the pain of childbirth to shattering glass ceilings, our resilience is the heart of our identity—an undying flame within us, always alight, always burning. This essential gut feeling that we have is tied to our intelligence and our strong analytical abilities. While our anatomy might be one significant aspect that differentiates men from women, it doesn't define our worth or our power. Our identities are shaped by a myriad of factors, including our socialization, cultural backgrounds, and individual experiences. In a world where there is gender equality, women can govern effectively. Our resilience knows no bounds, and our potential is limitless.

I intentionally entered this new world of aging with grace, dignity, unyielding determination, big fun, and a lot of joy, even in the absence of a sexual partner or male companion in my life. I navigated the winding roads of my life with fierce independence; I was in the driver's seat. In my solitude, much like a turtle that finds tranquility basking under the sun, I discovered empowerment rather than limitations. It was a realm of self-discovery, a tranquil harbor of introspection. I used my front door key, so abruptly returned to me as a catalyst to continue living without interruptions. It is never what happened to us in the past that matters. After all, things will happen when least expected. The winds of life are unpredictable, but we can set our sails. It is our actions—not our reactions—that count the most. Our stories are written in these decisions, shaping the narrative of our lives. When faced with a situation, we can act on it or react to it. By acting, I continued to enjoy life. Each day, a new canvas to paint my story on.

I created a new path by traveling with family and friends. These new adventures, like the turn of fresh pages in an exciting novel, added color and vibrancy to my life. I chose not to dwell in sorrow over not having a man in my life. This doesn't mean that sadness or grief isn't warranted— each of us processes the loss of a relationship differently. In my case, I found strength in forging my path ahead. I took control and, like a turtle, continued to move forward and never look back. Not once did I regret letting Clifford go. Even after Clifford's attempts at rekindling our relationship, I remained steadfast in my decision that our time together had run its course. I closed the chapter of my life with Clifford, firmly, but gently, with a softness reserved for past loves. Have I missed him sometimes? The answer is, of course, yes. He was the man who dried my tears after my husband Keith died. As such, there will always be a soft spot in my heart for my Clifford, but like a turtle resurfacing for a breath and diving back, I moved on with my life. Riding the waves of change, embracing the currents of new beginnings.

Inspired by the boundless potential I saw in the younger members of my family, we pooled our diverse talents in an ambitious quest to create a media company. A mosaic of creative minds coming together, a united front of boundless potential. Granted, I was a healthcare professional and never worked in the media. However, I found the world of media as mesmerizing as a painter before a fresh canvas, and as unpredictable as a tempest on a calm sea. I needed to understand the media's value regardless of my professional practice. Media in all its forms influences our lives, as I experienced firsthand when I was targeted on social media. After countless brainstorming sessions and late-night strategy meetings, my son, a few of my gifted nieces and nephews, and I officially formed the Vivens Media Group. Its mission was to create exciting content for podcasts, short films, books, and feature films. We were a diverse orchestra, each one of us playing our unique instrument, creating a harmonious symphony of ideas and creativity.

These bright, young people inspired me. Their dreams could become reality with financial backing and encouragement. I viewed myself as the champion of the group. Their dream was now my dream, and together we were a formidable force. Their dreams sparked a new vigor in me, their vibrant energy infusing me with a revitalizing sense of purpose and passion.

My son Kevin, who has over ten years of experience in corporate administration, holds a juris doctorate and a master's degree in business administration from George Washington University. His passion and dedication burn brightly. Joseph, an English major at Bowie State University, is the notable children's book author of *Chunky and Friends, The Candy Conundrum*, and *Juice and the Fountain of Youth*. A true literary artist and weaver of imaginative tales. Richard graduated from Queens College and shares his talent for videography and filmmaking with the group. Lynda is a Parsons School of Design alumna with years of expertise as a childrenswear and graphic designer. Her creativity knows no bounds. Ingrid is a graduate of John Jay College who majored in criminal justice and psychology. She is also a poet and short story writer. Francesca holds a master's degree in education leadership and administration from Argosy University, helping companies progress with next-level digital processes. Finally, my grandson Keith, a journalism major at Arizona State University and the youngest member of our team, is our intern; he provides insights and understanding to our "Gen Z" viewpoints and future project goals. Together, we became the board of directors of "Vivens Media Group."

Even though the media world was utterly unfamiliar to me, like a foreign language being learned, I wanted to participate and enjoy it as if I were a millennial. This new challenge invigorated me. Working with these young people allowed me to accomplish that goal. I recruited a personal assistant to help me navigate social media. My compass in this sea of hashtags and likes, Fanie became my go-to resource for social media. In addition to having a beautiful disposition with me as a senior and a newbie with social media, she accompanied me on trips to ensure that my in-person presentations went smoothly. She was the perfect, steadfast companion on my new media voyage.

My personal goal with the Vivens Media Group was to educate myself in the media world while also giving those gifted young people in my family the opportunity to see their ideas come to fruition and leave a lasting impression on their audiences. A seed of ambition, watered with diligence and care, ready to bloom.

As it turned out, Vivens Media saved my publishing ambitions at a crucial juncture. Their support was like the lighthouse guiding a ship through a tumultuous storm. Unexpectedly, I became the company's biggest customer with the publication of my book, an accomplishment that echoed through the halls of my life. I was ecstatic when a prestigious company like Atlantic Publishing agreed to publish my book. A dream written in the stars, now a reality. Vivens Media was present to negotiate a contract every step of the way, each negotiation a dance in the grand ballroom of opportunity. After a few meetings, the publishing house and I, the author, ultimately agreed to a highly successful contract. I proved my tenacity, continuing to push forward despite the unpredictable waves of the publishing industry. My spirit, a tower of strength, relentless and unwavering.

I made it clear to Atlantic that a reputable editor had thoroughly revised my manuscript; the text was ready to be published. Each word, each line, had been meticulously honed and polished, the raw material of my thoughts and experiences shaped into a manuscript of gleaming gems. Obviously, Atlantic as a business made it clear to Vivens Media that they had publishing standards they must follow. An agreement etched in the stone of professionalism. They informed me that my manuscript might require additional editing to meet industry standards. I agreed, on the condition that I would have the right to approve the final edited copy before printing. My story, my words, my truth, carefully crafted and preserved.

My agreement to a rewrite was made solely to comply with their rules and regulations. I saw it as a necessary hurdle, a part of the roller coaster ride that was my journey to publication. The go-to person assigned to my project by Atlantic was a manager who was only supposed to make minor modifications to comply with Atlantic Publishing Company's standards. The morning of our flight back to the United States from Bangkok, Thailand, Christina and I were still in our room when I received a copy of the revised manuscript from my Atlantic designated manager. I erupted into a joyful yell.

"OMG, Christina! Christina, Chica! I just got a copy of the book." The words poured from my lips, jubilant, bouncing with the joy of a thousand suns. I was screaming. "Get up! Get up!" In my excitement, I ripped away the protective shroud of sleep, the crisp sheets crumpled under my insistent tug. I pulled the bed linen off her face. I was ecstatic, and she couldn't care less. My dear friend and traveling companion, without opening her eyes, whispered, "Chica," as we call each other, "go back to sleep."

"You don't understand, Chica. This is from the Atlantic publishing company! I have the book. Get up," I yelled once more.

The words burst out of me. I had been patient and persistent, my spirit fueled by tenacious hope, and now I was holding the results of that perseverance in my hands. My heart hammered in my chest, a wild drum echoing my triumph.

I took a deep breath, trying to still the rapid beating of my heart and control my overwhelming excitement.

Once she finally woke up, we finished packing, our belongings neatly tucked away like treasured memories, ate breakfast, and went to the hotel's business center to print a paper copy of what was now the book for me to read on the flight. Despite all the technological progress I had made, I still preferred reading from my paper copy than directly from the computer. I enjoyed the old-school charm of paper under my fingers, the smell of ink and binding glue, the rustle of pages as they turned. I craved the tactile affirmation of my achievement. I wanted a copy in my hand to touch and feel in the airplane.

I was finally at the airport, ready for my twenty-plus hour trip back to America. As I settled into the plush seat of my first-class cabin, my heart raced with anticipation. I reached into my bag and pulled out the fruits of my labor—my manuscript, now exceeding two hundred pages. I held it in my hands, its weight a satisfying testament to the hard work and countless hours that went into its creation.

As I read, I couldn't believe what lay before me. Each word felt like a jab, each sentence a gut punch. The manuscript was completely rewritten, marred by misspellings, incorrect punctuation, and even a jumbled storyline and factual errors. Christina stared at me, concern knitting her brows. She insisted, adamant, "Give me the pages you've read, Chica. Let me help you." I didn't want her to read this text because it was so poorly written. She could not compare and contrast Atlantic's manuscript with the document provided to the publishing company. Her pitiful gaze met mine, reflecting the distress mirrored on my own face. I know I must have looked helpless. Silent tears streamed down my cheeks. I was so hurt.

For a moment, I felt as vulnerable as a turtle flipped on its back. But I knew I had to be valiant and right myself to continue this journey. I steeled my spirit for the battle ahead.

"Chica," she said once again. "I can help you; you know that my company does marketing. Let me read it," she firmly insisted.

Without uttering another word, I gathered all the pages I had read with rage that threatened to consume me like wildfire and reluctantly handed them to her in despair. Each page felt heavy with betrayal as I passed them over.

We were both gasping, our breaths hitched in a symphony of disbelief, outraged at how the content had been changed to reflect a stereotypically negative image of a black woman. It was offensive and humiliating. The sting of injustice was like a mouthful of bitter herbs. I was reading a text so alien, it bore no resemblance to the manuscript I had lovingly crafted and entrusted to this company. Even my father's name was misspelled, an egregious error that stung like a fresh wound, proving that the changes must have been made intentionally.

As I fought through the upset, wading through the swamp of emotions, I reminded myself of the turtle's perseverance and determination to keep moving forward, regardless of the obstacles.

I thought back to my time as a freshman in my nursing program, where I'd scored in the ninety-eighth percentile despite English being my second language. Impressed by my exceptional performance, my nursing school principal had forwarded my grades to the licensing board in Albany, New York. Given the strength of my academic record, they granted me a license to practice as a Licensed Practical Nurse without the usual requirement of taking the State Board Exam. According to Atlantic's document, though, I'd somehow dropped from the top of my class to the bottom. They'd stolen my academic laurels and replaced them with thorns of deception.

The revised document was almost unrecognizable, riddled with glaring inaccuracies. For instance, in reality, I had been pregnant with my son at thirty one, well after I had earned my baccalaureate degree in nursing. However, the document from Atlantic Publishing Company that I was reading on the airplane stated that I had been pregnant at thirteen. There were several contradictions, hundreds of hyphenated words, and countless grammatical or spelling mistakes. The frustration I felt was as hot as a bonfire, every new error another log on the flame. It was a direct sabotage of my manuscript. Each error felt like a stone weighing down a turtle, slowing its progress, a relentless burden I was determined to shrug off.

The text inexplicably concluded with a dog charity page, a stark departure from my story. This unrelated addition felt like an invasion into my carefully curated narrative. This dog story had been added without my permission. The white female manager editing my manuscript informed me that Atlantic Publishing Company included this dog charity page in all of their books as a demonstration of their support for animals. The irrelevance stung, like salt on a fresh wound, adding to the travesty of it all. I wanted to satisfy my curiosity. To outsmart her, I requested two samples of books that Atlantic had already published to assess the paper quality and weight used to print my book.

In the face of these challenges, staring down the beast of betrayal, I held onto the turtle's wisdom, which told me to stand firm, remain calm, and be patient.

She was unaware that my primary motivation was to catch them in their lie—this supposed ubiquitous "dog narrative" closing page was curiously absent from all other books. Both books lacked the dog charity page, as was to be expected. However, this black woman's book was set to close with a photo of a dog-related charity commercial. Go figure! A bitter chuckle escaped my lips as the irony settled in.

Like a turtle weathering the storm, I summoned a stubborn resolve to withstand the challenges.

I had a pressing deadline to have a physical book by Christmas week. On March 9th, I was to launch my book at a sold-out, very significant luncheon in Florida. I called my publishing manager from the car, driving away from the airport, to convey my disappointment. She found it difficult to comprehend why I was so irate and frustrated.

I insisted vehemently that the manuscript needed to be rewritten from scratch.

I imagined the manuscript as an old, tattered map that needed to be redrawn, its once-golden edges now frayed and dull. She didn't think twice about telling me that if the manuscript needed to be re-edited, her company couldn't deliver on time for the March 9th launch. The manuscript became my cardiac arrest patient that I needed to resuscitate.

With the tenacity of a turtle, I committed to reviving my manuscript.

Christina and I worked tirelessly for over forty hours at her house, determined to restore my manuscript. Our fingers danced across the keyboards of three desktop computers. We showed the perseverance of sea turtles battling through the sand to reach the ocean. Each monitor was displaying a different document: the original manuscript I'd provided Atlantic, the publishing company's flawed text, and a freshly edited copy.

I sent an updated version of my newly edited manuscript to Atlantic with the caveat that no printing be carried out without my final permission. My trust in this company had eroded to a point beyond any reconciliation. Before hundreds of copies of this travesty could be printed, I demanded a sample book. I completed the requested print permission form from Atlantic with one caveat that the final five or so mistakes highlighted in the sample paperback copy be corrected before the final print of one hundred books was made.

The doorbell rang, marking the long-awaited day of book delivery. I was ecstatic that my dream of publishing my memoir had come true. I tore open a box as I shouted, "The books are here! The books are here!" The words bounced off the walls and echoed through the house, like a song of victory, loud enough for my assistant, who was at the house, to run outside and join me in opening the five boxes of books that had been delivered in front of my garage door.

I posed for a photo with the boxes since I was so delighted. The book cover page was so beautiful I was smiling and joyful as I took a book out of the box.

I was like a child with a new toy. My heart pounded with anticipation, the rhythm a wild, exultant drumroll. I eagerly opened the book to the specific pages to ensure that the remaining few mistakes in the sample paperback book had been corrected. To my horror, not one correction was made. I had one hundred books full of errors, and the Florida book launch was just days away.

After shedding blood, sweat, and tears to produce this book, I was so close but so far. The unattended errors were a glaring act of negligence—or even sabotage— and the disregard for my explicit instructions was mind-boggling. Seeking an explanation for the myriad of mistakes, I reached out to anyone at the company who would talk to me. Their responses ranged from dismissive to apologetic, but none provided a satisfactory answer to the question: was the company incompetent, spiteful, or both? I faced each challenge head-on, refusing to be swept away.

Being persistent and never giving up is one of the twenty-five rules in *Girls Can Move Mountains*. I had to put into practice one of my own rules. Challenges are a part of life, and it is through challenges that we grow and develop. Atlantic Publishing was able to make the needed corrections. My determination had been resolute and unyielding, moving forward like a steam train powering up a steep incline regardless of the bumps along the way.

I finally had one hundred perfect paperback books for the launch of March 9th, 2020. The book release was thrilling. The location was exquisitely and culturally decorated by the Cle Haitian Ladies Network, like a resplendent tropical paradise, the colors and textures of the room as rich and diverse as the pages of my book. They sponsored a women's empowerment luncheon to welcome me to South Florida and showcase my book.

To commemorate the occasion, a Caribbean television station was present at the event. There were singers, drummers, and dancers, each one adding a brushstroke to the kaleidoscopic canvas of the event, and the food was delicious. Many women who attended the event left with books, indicating that the book was well received. I carried my accomplishments with pride, relieved that my journey had borne fruit.

I did not let my audience down. I performed well, never disclosing the obstacles I had to overcome or the countless mountains I had to move to be at their event with books in hand. The slogan "Girls Can Move Mountains" was on banners and large screens, and all the tables had books. It was a testament to the turtle-like purposefulness that I had embodied throughout this journey.

Behind every successful woman is herself—her own dignity, grace, and determination. The ambition, the drive, the unwavering attitude, and the courage to move mountains despite the daily obstacles we face can be staggering. Facing these challenges can feel like climbing a mountain. Success is invigorating, a rush of pure elation. Every one of us experiences those life-testing moments when all we want to do is give up, wash our hands, and quit.

Sister, that's when it is most vital for you to listen to that murmur of your inner voice that says, "There is gold at the end of the tunnel. Take a deep breath, move like a turtle, taste success, and walk like you have diamonds at the meeting of your thighs. And with your head high, just keep on going." Like the little choo choo train, verbally and out loud convince yourself by repeating over and over, "I think I can, I think I can, I think I can," because yes, you can. Just as a turtle doesn't second guess its instinct to reach the sea, you too shouldn't second guess your ability to reach your goals.

Eventually, those mountains will be almost invisible in your rearview mirror, like I finally had books to share. They had become little more than hiccups in my journey, a testament to the adaptability and determination that had led me to this moment. *Girls Can Move Mountains* has been published in three languages and available on Audible. And just as the core values of humanity remain constant, the message of my book is consistent across all languages.

Turtle Wisdom: Fight for Your Narrative

Just as a turtle bravely pushes through the sandy shore, not swayed by the odds stacked against it, we too can demonstrate unwavering tenacity in our lives. There were instances when my own life's narrative, the saga intricately penned down in my memoir, was tampered and twisted by a disgruntled woman. This act painted an inaccurate, stereotypical image of me. But, akin to a turtle's resolve, I decided to fight back, reclaim my narrative, and maintain the authenticity of my identity. This embodies the essence of courage and standing up for the truth—a lesson straight from the life of a turtle.

At different stages in our lives, we face unique challenges that test our strength and resolve. It might be the feeling of being misunderstood, or seeing your words and actions taken out of context, or even having your very identity called into question. In these trying times, it's beneficial to embrace the turtle's wisdom—to persist, assert, and never surrender. Take the reins of your narrative. Always remember that you hold the authority and the right to script and tell your own story.

TURTLE INSIGHTS

1. Has there ever been a situation where you felt that someone else was hijacking your narrative? What was your response?

2. How can you take back control of your narrative when it's being misrepresented or misinterpreted?

3. Can you recall an instance where you defended your beliefs, even though it was challenging? How did this experience influence your emotions?

4. In what ways can you integrate the lesson of the turtle's unwavering courage and persistence into your day-to-day life?

5. Are there certain stereotypes or misconceptions that you feel have influenced how others perceive you? How can you strategize to alter these perceptions?

AFFIRMATIONS

- I am the author of my own story, and I have the power to shape my narrative.

- My voice matters, and my experiences are valid.

- I have the confidence and courage to stand up against adversity and to fight for my truth.

- I am more than the stereotypes or misconceptions that others may have of me.

- Like a turtle, I have the strength to persist, endure, and move forward, no matter the challenges I face.

CHAPTER NINE

It's Social Media Marketing Time

My niece Ingrid had the opportunity to read the first draft of *Girls Can Move Mountains*, absorbing the raw, transformative energy before it was officially published. She was anxious to see the finished product. Being out of state, she had eagerly ordered five copies of the book from Amazon, her mind filled with visions of sharing the empowering manifesto with her close-knit group of girlfriends.

One Saturday afternoon, I had a house full of family members celebrating my niece Natalie's birthday, who just so happened to have been in transit in Florida on her birthday while traveling abroad. A delicious aroma of freshly baked cake wafted in the air mingling with bursts of hearty laughter and warm wishes. In the middle of the celebration, my phone rang. It was a frantic call from Ingrid. Her voice, trembling with distress, conveyed her concern about the lack of content in the five books she had purchased from Amazon—the last page of each volume ended with a coma at page one hundred and forty-four.

It was clear that something had gone astray. I clarified to her that the last page of the books I had received from the publishing company ended at page two hundred and eighty-one with a period at the end. The discrepancy stood out glaringly. Since I had not ordered any books from Amazon, I was unaware of the incompleteness of the books she received. Realizing the severity of the situation, I, as the author, sincerely apologized and reassured her that I would address the issue with the publishing company on Monday. My carefully crafted work had been swept away from its intended audience, and a pang of worry wriggled its way into my heart.

Early on Sunday morning, my friend Clifford called me. He was bewildered and a bit irate because the eleven books he had ordered for his colleagues at the law firm were incomplete, ending abruptly at page one hundred and forty-four. I found myself in a position where I had to explain the unfortunate Amazon error, taking time with each caller to reassure them, promising that their incomplete books would be promptly replaced. I was on damage-control mode, a skill I possessed from past experiences. As an executive, I had to write the policy and procedure for damage control and model handling mishaps in our own company. Each word of reassurance I spoke was like applying a bandage on a wound.

In my book *Girls Can Move Mountains,* I titled a chapter "Sweet and Sour," discussing my life's simultaneous highs and lows. This Amazon episode was no different. A dash of salt in the sweet soup of success. I grew up accepting that even amid my greatest joy, there will always be a catastrophe. Since things happen to people every day, I had to learn to adapt to that reality. I came to believe that what matters in life is not the unexpected event but how we handle the unexpected events that appear out of nowhere, like the one in my one-hundred-and-forty-four-page book drama.

This turn of events hit me like a gust of unexpected wind, leaving me momentarily breathless. I had not seen this coming. And the way we respond to these kinds of circumstances determines our survival. Like a turtle, quick to retract into its shell at the sign of danger, I realized I had to adapt quickly to this sudden shift, ready myself for what was to come. It's a dance with unpredictability, a tango with fate. Do we let the event dictate how we react, or do we manage it by exercising control? By taking action, we stay in charge of the circumstance and improve our chances of succeeding. Reacting often causes us to lose control, making it easier for others to manipulate and take charge of the situation. I always push myself to maintain my composure and seize control of the situation.

Drawing upon a history of navigating calamities with this company, I decided to handle this scenario my way—being kind but forceful. I recalled the countless negotiation meetings and damage control situations, where I had learned that firmness often brings results faster than anger. Navigating this choppy sea, I knew my exterior needed to be tough while I maintained an inner sense of patience and calm. I needed to figure out what caused this stray bullet that struck me yet one more time. I found myself wondering whether this was sabotage or an honest mistake. If it was sabotage, what could possibly be the motive? The mystery gnawed at my patience. My inquiring mind wanted to know. Yet another humiliating setback was testing me, but this was just a continuation of my battle with this publishing company. I decided to stop being polite. My patience, once as endless as a tranquil sea, began to storm.

It was clear that these repeated, well-calculated, deliberate actions required strength, grace, and poise. It was time to assert myself fully, to show the strength and determination behind the name Solanges—that "s" at the end of my name was about to make its significance known. In French, an "s" at the end of a word indicates that the word is plural. In the case of my name, I like to say that there are two sides to me—there's the Solanges you interact with daily and the one who scares the hell out of me when she comes out. Atlantic was about to meet the other side of Solanges—the one who stands up for herself, fights for her rights, and doesn't back down from a challenge. I had two days to cool off and plan my strategy. It was a battle brewing, and I was ready to bring the heat.

Monday morning, I inquired about the origin of the Amazon debacle. I discovered that Amazon and the publishing company are parties to a contract whereby Atlantic electronically transfers manuscripts to Amazon for printing and sales by Amazon. Atlantic assured me that an investigation would be conducted, and I would be given a response as soon as it became available. With patience and steadfastness, I found solace in my own internal fortress of resilience. It was a waiting game now, a suspenseful standoff. I waited, trusting that my shell was sturdy enough to weather whatever outcome resulted from the investigation. I was kind, understanding, and patient, yet concerned. In nursing school, I learned always to be nice but firm when dealing with psychiatric patients. I was handling the issues with Atlantic Publishing with the same approach I used when dealing with my psychiatric patients: patience, firmness, and resolve. My resolve was as unshakeable as a mountain. I was nice and firm while I waited for an explanation. The stage was set, with me on one side, and Atlantic Publishing on the other. Now, all we needed was the climax of this peculiar drama.

It's crucial to remember that verbal conversation fades away. Almost every phone conversation I had with my Atlantic manager, in relation to the intentionally ruined manuscript, was documented in writing. During Christmas week, my marketing manager, Christina, spent forty hours fixing issues in my manuscript. I had to compensate her with a couple of thousands of dollars for her time and effort. Almost everyone whose email address I had at Atlantic Publishing, including the executive director, was copied on correspondences that were crucial to my case. Like pieces of a puzzle clicking into place, these letters laid the groundwork for my battle. As the issues continued to spiral, threatening to engulf our young company, Vivens Media Group, we knew we needed more than our own resources. We decided to retain a media law firm, seeking their expertise and support to navigate this storm.

Drawing from a deep reservoir of strength and the wisdom gained from past encounters, I found my way amidst the chaos. I confirmed my suspicion that Atlantic Publishing was the source of the incomplete book with only one hundred and forty-four pages. Amazon had no means of knowing that Atlantic uploaded an incomplete file into their system. What they had obtained from Atlantic Publishing was what was printed and sold. As such, it was not an Amazon issue. Once the error was acknowledged, Atlantic Publishing uploaded a new complete manuscript to Amazon. A wave of relief washed over me, but it was mixed with a lingering frustration that such a mishap could have happened in the first place. New books were printed and shipped out. I immediately replaced books for certain Amazon customers from my hundred books. I have no idea how many others received the incomplete, one-hundred-and-forty-four-page version of the book. And I don't know how many never received a replacement with the complete two hundred and eighty-one pages.

I tenaciously safeguarded my work and reputation. I held my ground. I had an adrenaline rush throughout my body, and myriad of questions were competing in my brain. I was puzzled and wanted to know what had happened. Was it an error or an extension of the evil deeds of the Atlantic manager? And if it was malicious, why? This badass girl had a curious mind and wanted answers to all her questions. I didn't back down; instead of reacting, I took action by holding the publishing house accountable. Once they realized that I had them by the throat, they had no choice but to figure out a way to make me whole.

The turtle teaches us that slow and steady wins the race, and in this publishing saga, I embodied that very essence. I embraced the relief that came with the resolution. Unexpectedly and without a formal request, I received a "canceling contract with the author" letter from Atlantic with no strings attached. By this action, Atlantic accepted responsibility for how my case was handled. I was free to engage with a different publisher. I was relieved to have been released from this publishing agreement. I was happy that Atlantic acknowledged how one of its staff had mishandled my case and took the proper action to make the client whole. I subsequently published the book through our own Vivens Media Company.

Having been an employer in a business of over eight hundred individuals, I can say with certainty that any company's personnel can make the company a five-star business or destroy its reputation, as in this case. I do not believe that Atlantic as a company is bad; it just so happened that they had a disgruntled employee. Given a different manager, my experience could have been different. Apart from my manager, everyone at Atlantic treated me with respect and expressed sympathy for the turmoil. I wanted to believe this misfortune was a unique experience for this company.

This individual modified my manuscript, misrepresenting my accomplishments by dropping them from the ninety-eighth percentile to the nineteen percentile in my nursing school program—a change that could have affected my credibility. Additionally, she misspelled my father's name, further displaying a lack of professionalism and attention to detail. She was the one who altered my manuscript, changing my age during pregnancy from thirty-one to thirteen—a distortion that fed into harmful stereotypes about black women. The same Atlantic manager who modified my manuscript and misspelled my father's name was also responsible for uploading the first hundred books to the printer, complete with several uncorrected mistakes. I insisted, and they agreed that those one hundred books were to be corrected and reprinted at the expense of the Atlantic publishing company.

She knowingly submitted the incomplete manuscript for printing and sales on Amazon. The actions of this manager, both in regard to her job responsibilities and her treatment of me—a black woman who had overcome substantial obstacles—were highly unprofessional and discriminatory. She could not deal with my success story and maliciously sabotaged it. She may have been angry with her boss, and I may have been her perfect victim for revenge. I ended up feeling sorry for her. I wish I had the opportunity to guide and redirect her negative energy.

There's a lesson in the turtle's slow and steady approach—it illustrates the power of perseverance and determination. If she, and other young women facing similar challenges, would learn to embrace these attributes, they too could move mountains. She needed to understand that young women like her also possess the power to overcome adversity and succeed. This is a journey of self-reflection and honesty, which I have explored in *Girls Can Move Mountains*. A lack of self-love can become destructive, as in her case. One must love oneself to be happy. Tell the girl in the mirror how much you love her. After I received the cancellation of my contract with Atlantic, I learned that she was no longer an employee of the publishing company. Regrettably, she decided to resolve her personal issues with her employer by projecting her anger toward a black woman she had never met. Due to her reactive nature instead of a proactive approach, she ended up on the losing side in this scenario—a clear example of the potential consequences of impulsivity.

Throughout my fifty-year career in healthcare, I've witnessed the fallout of impulsive actions. Like the Atlantic manager, many individuals have lost their jobs as a consequence. The Atlantic manager's situation was a similar case of reacting impulsively rather than responding thoughtfully. Ultimately, I must admit that I was never told if she left voluntarily or was removed. All I was told was that she was no longer with the company. By taking calculated, deliberate actions, I was able to extricate myself from this troubling situation, completely unburdened by any lingering obligations or issues.

In a successful ending to a challenging chapter, *Girls Can Move Mountains* was ultimately published by our company, Vivens Media Group, a testament to the power of definitive action over impulsive reaction. Every negative has a tiny bit of positivity; it is our job to locate and use it to our advantage. I never assumed the role of the victim and never felt sorry for Solanges. Instead, I always have a fighter's mindset. I think my high level of curiosity and can-do attitude had a lot to do with how I was able to go from being a poor little Haitian girl who came to America on a two-month visa, not speaking a word of English, to becoming a business owner, a force to be reckoned with, an author and an international public speaker.

Drawing inspiration from the turtle's humble and steady nature, I learned always to keep my eyes open and I'm constantly aware of when to speak and when to keep my mouth shut. Only when I thought I could win did I decide to argue my case. I wouldn't debate with someone who lacks the maturity and the capacity to handle the argument. If it does not impact my life or well-being, I am content to let others believe they have won. Staff members would frequently turn to me after a meeting or a complex family interaction and ask, "How did you do it? Why did you allow her to get away with it?" "Why not?" I would respond. "What would it benefit me to argue with her? It would be ineffective and a waste of energy."

My relatives and friends were perplexed by the degree of control I exercised over the manager at Atlantic Publishing. She had an issue, not me. My job was to make sure that I was treated fairly. She had a responsibility to me and her employer, both of which she failed, resulting in the loss of her employment.

As a tennis player, I know that a tennis match can only be won by just one player, regardless of how well both competitors are playing. This situation is no different during an argument or a debate. I was on a battlefield with the manager of the publishing company, I played to win, and I succeeded. Life is a theater where we perform our parts as actors and actresses regularly. I maintain the authority to reposition individuals in my theater of life, from the nosebleed to the orchestra seats, based on their behavior, our relationship, and personal interactions.

I choose who enters my theater, and I decide where they sit. I can always control myself, but I cannot control them. I learned to manage what I can, and I ask God to grant me the serenity to accept the things I cannot change, the courage to change, support and guide those that I can, like my new twenty-four-year-old friend from Boston that I was able to mentor. I prayed for wisdom to recognize when there are individuals whom I cannot change, support, or help, such as the inexperienced manager from Atlantic Publishing Company.

Reading Les Brown's autobiography instilled in me the drive to realize my aspirations and emboldened me to embrace my authentic self. I hope that my story, told in *Girls Can Move Mountains,* can inspire others, whether a young woman in her twenties or a middle-aged woman facing struggles. I hope they can find in my journey the same inspiration I discovered in Les Brown's *Live Your Dream* as a young adult. Life is too short to allow anyone or anything to spoil your joy.

After overcoming all the obstacles presented by Atlantic Publishing, I proudly put my book—a testament to resilience—up for sale on social media and into libraries for students to discover. Life is richer and more rewarding when you believe in your power to overcome obstacles, to move your own mountains.

Turtle Wisdom: Persevere through Challenges

The voyage to publishing a book can be fraught with hurdles and setbacks, much like the journey of a turtle swimming against robust tides. During the publishing process, there were instances where we came up against challenges that seemed insurmountable. Yet, mirroring the resilient spirit of the turtle, we drew inspiration to persevere and push through. Each challenging situation called for us to seize control, maintain our stance, and refuse to allow external circumstances dictate our final result.

This narrative serves as a testament to the invincible power of purpose in our lives. Life may throw us curveballs and construct roadblocks in our path, but it's our reaction to these difficulties that defines us. While reacting often leaves us feeling out of control, taking deliberate action puts us in the driver's seat, allowing us to steer the situation to our benefit, much like a turtle doggedly battling the water current. This instills the reminder that we are indeed the sculptors of our own destiny and that we possess the capacity to transform challenges into stepping stones.

TURTLE INSIGHTS

1. Reflect on an occasion when you reacted impulsively instead of consciously taking the reins. If given a chance to revisit that moment, what would your approach be?

2. How has adversity shaped you into a stronger individual? Can you pinpoint the "turtle moments" in your life where perseverance played a pivotal role?

3. What personal characteristics have aided you in weathering storms, and how can you nurture these traits further?

4. Can you recollect an instance where you consciously chose to maintain your calm and patience amidst a challenging situation? How did this affect the outcome?

5. When confronted with challenges, do you typically view yourself as a victim or a fighter? Why is that?

AFFIRMATIONS

- I am the architect of my destiny. I opt to seize control and take action rather than merely react.

- I embody adaptability and can withstand any storm that life throws my way, just like a turtle boldly swimming against the tide.

- I perceive obstacles as disguised opportunities, providing a platform for me to evolve and fortify my goals.

- In the face of adversity, I hold on to my control, navigating through it with unwavering patience and determination.

- Like an unstoppable force of nature, I relentlessly advance against any current, conquer any mountain that blocks my path.

CHAPTER TEN

Reconnecting with My Roots

While in America, amid the shimmering skyscrapers and ceaseless hum of city life, I realized fairly quickly that if you can't beat them, you had to figure out a way to join them and that education was everything. Through the years, in addition to getting degrees and working in prestigious hospitals and nursing homes—each a hive of knowledge and medical prowess—I created a path for me to become successful. I married a non-Creole-speaking intellectual, a tall, dark, and handsome gentleman with a keen intellect that matched his striking exterior who was instrumental in the person I became.

I partnered with two caucasian millionaires to form a company—an adventurous leap into the pulsing heart of the business world. I joined major boards and commissions and was elected officer at state and national associations. Each achievement was another bright and colorful feather in my well-decorated cap. I used legal consultants from reputable law firms. My taxes and banking services were from well-known companies. I learned it was not who you know that matters but who knows *you* that makes a difference—a revelation that echoed powerfully in my eager mind.

I observed how the top professionals in my field navigated their careers, and I replicated their success, adding a touch of class and zest. I danced through this new landscape with a rhythm and vitality all my own. I would often be in major company assemblies and the only minority in the room. A singular drop of ink in a sea of blank paper. I always felt like I was at the right place at the right time. Never did I feel that I did not belong. On the contrary, I saw myself as equal to or better than others as we shared the same oxygen in the room. It was as though I was painting over the plain canvas of my past with the bold, vibrant colors of newfound self-identity and ambition.

Having chosen that path to build my success, I was not deliberately distancing myself from my Haitian roots. It was mainly due to circumstances and the environment in which I was operating—like a boat on the open sea, adjusting its course with the changing winds.

I was around other Caribbean individuals but very few Haitians. My husband was educated British since he was from the island of Barbados and worked at the Organization of American States, then at the International Telecommunications Satellite Organization; as such, we were surrounded not only by Caribbean islanders but Asians, Latinos, and Africans from the continent of Africa, with few representatives from Haiti. My ties to my Haitian roots were tenuous at best, limited to sparse family gatherings that served as bittersweet reminders of my cultural heritage, stirring a longing within me that was both melancholic and oddly comforting. My sisters would jokingly say that I spoke Creole just as though it was my second language.

I was ecstatic when I was invited to attend a Haitian women's luncheon at the Haitian Embassy in Washington, D.C. A symphony of familiar faces, accents, and culture awaited me—a promise of home. It was the first time in a long time that I was in the presence of so many individuals of Haitian descent, women at that. Bathing in the grand atmosphere of the embassy—a stately manor radiating with the dignity and pride of my homeland, the aroma of familiar spices in the air, and the hum of Creole conversations surrounding me—I felt a piece of home had found me.

I will never forget the spread of delicious Haitian food on the buffet table—the rich aroma, the vibrant colors, and the distinctive taste of each dish. Each bite was a nostalgic journey, transporting me back to my youth. The potent flavors evoked tales of my homeland, whispering stories of a past I cherished. I did not know most of the women. However, I still felt at home and somewhat familiar in their presence—like a sweet melody hummed in the background. Every year I continued to attend this luncheon and became more comfortable and appreciative of the sisterhood being developed—a flourishing garden of shared roots, experiences, and dreams. As I grew closer to these wonderful women, forming many friendships along the way, I found myself in a position where I could offer suggestions to the steering committee.

In 2013, I was on the cover of the *Washington Women's Magazine*.

I carried at least fifty copies of the magazine to share with my fellow Haitian sisters. Unfortunately, I was denied the opportunity by the leader of the group, who informed me that they did not allow marketing or advertising at the luncheon. With a heavy heart and a sense of rejection I hadn't expected, I returned home, my box of untouched magazines a silent testament to my disappointment. I continued to attend and offer advice, never giving up.

I persistently encouraged Nadine, the steering committee chairperson, to recognize the potential in our group of Haitian women and to diversify our gatherings beyond just the annual luncheon. I could see the boundless potential in this tapestry of vibrant lives. Finally, the group made a thrilling decision—to organize a symposium, extending our usual luncheon into a weekend-long celebration of shared heritage and collective wisdom. It was a momentous leap forward, a turning point promising a new level of connection and impact. It was like watching a lotus bloom—a new beginning of something beautiful. Unexpectedly, on the last day of the conference, Nadine invited me to the stage to deliver the closing remarks.

I recall sharing that I hired an average of about eight hundred people in my business, yet, due to language barriers and a lack of established networks, I found it challenging to communicate these vacancies to my well-qualified Haitian sisters. I was acutely aware of the vast sea of opportunity that lay before us, yet I felt like a captain without a ship, unable to steer my Haitian sisters toward these promising horizons. Without giving it a second thought, I shifted my focus from the audience and spoke to Nadine as if we were the only two in the room. In this moment of shared spotlight, a new path was being carved.

I was in awe that such a group existed, considering my entry to America when I felt so alone and lonely. How I wish such a group existed in my days. I wanted Haitian women to value the sisterhood that was being created. So I pledged $10,000 for a directory and an additional $10,000 for the next three consecutive years to ensure this was not the first and last symposium. I was genuinely impressed and wanted to see more events from this group.

As the Haitian Ladies Network started to blossom, it was clear that a more modern approach to membership was needed. Instead of a traditional directory, we turned to social media. This strategy paid off, as our follower count quickly exploded to between thirty and fifty thousand members. It was like watching a firework burst into the night sky—vivid, awe-inspiring, and full of potential. They nicknamed me the godmother of the Haitian Ladies Network, an honor that filled my heart with warmth and pride.

My gesture, a token of pure love, had no hidden expectations for a return on investment. Yet I was embraced by this cohesive, powerful group of women when I published my book *Girls Can Move Mountains*. Haitian Ladies Network was the first to create an international event, even during the Covid 19 pandemic, to blast my book worldwide. I credit this network of sisterhood for the success of my book. I will forever be grateful to my

Haitian Ladies Network of DC. This launch was watched around the world. Books were ordered as far away as Prague. Doing a good deed, I've found, not only brings a sense of personal satisfaction, but also often yields unexpected rewards—if not in this life, then surely in the next.

SOLANGES AND NADINE DUPLESSY-KEARNS

Lao Tzu, an ancient Chinese philosopher, once said, "The journey of a thousand miles, starts with a single step."

Eighteen years ago, Nadine, a petite yet mighty woman, new to the Washington DC area, took the first step of inviting a few new acquaintances of her same Haitian cultural background to lunch. This small luncheon grew into a majestic annual event called the Haitian Ladies Network: Igniting Our Power" networking weekend every October. At our last gathering, which took place in October 2023, I was once again an ardent sponsor, partner, and lifelong supporter of HLN. I was elated to be a speaker at the symposium and proud of the growth and strength of this organization. The Future is truly Female.

The Haitian Ladies in South Florida were also having major events with the book launch. I recall "The CLE Haitian Sisters"' were the first to have had a sold-out function in Miami with theatrical performances, Haitian drummers, and even a Haitian television station to broadcast the event. The invitations just continued to come for me to speak and share the book. Accompanied by my personal assistant Fanie, I presented my book at the Ayiti Community Trust annual gala fundraiser in Little Haiti.

I received enthusiastic feedback and sparking important discussions about women's empowerment.

Because of this major support from my Haitian sisters, I became a sought-after speaker in the South Florida area and beyond. I was invited to speak via Zoom due to the Covid epidemic at Broward College, Miami Dade College, Maryland University, and others. I spoke regularly on podcasts and Zoom meetings, reaching women near and far. On a podcast, a young woman wrote in the chat, "Can you help me find my voice?" I pledged that I would find her and offer my help.

Through her electronic detective work, Fanie found this twenty-four-year-old woman in Boston. It was like a digital hunt through the forest of the world wide web, and we found our precious gem. We talked for hours by phone and developed a mentor-mentee relationship. Like the master and apprentice, we began our journey together. I helped her to move from where she was in life at that moment to a place where she became very proud of the girl in the mirror. It was like watching a caterpillar transform into a beautiful butterfly, right before my eyes. In 2022, she attended the Haitian Ladies Network Symposium in Washington, D.C., and I had the pleasure of having her as my house guest in Maryland. It was as if the pages of our digital bond had finally come to life.

The first time I laid eyes on her in person was when she arrived at the front door of my condo. Her eyes twinkled with an undying spirit as she shared her plans and goals, a clear testament to her determination and tenacity. Her smile, ever present even in the face of challenges, was as infectious as the joy that danced in her heart. She had clear dreams and a plan for her journey; all she needed was someone to guide her on the right path. Over the course of the symposium's long weekend, we bonded over shared experiences, discussions about our homeland, and the mutual challenges we faced as Haitian sisters.

I was able to help my Boston sister to move some steep mountains that were in her way. She took calculated risks, made gutsy decisions, and emerged victorious. Her accomplishments filled me with pride. She had arrived at her destination, her journey with my guidance concluded.

The Haitian Ladies Network of DC has indeed managed to connect Haitian women from all over the world. This is a testament to the power of belief and imagination. While most people say, "I'll believe it when I see it," I say, "I believed it and then imagined it." Haitian Ladies Network of DC was just what I saw when I was nagging Nadine to do more with the group. They are now internationally Igniting Haitian Ladies Power. They are the pride and joy of their godmother.

Much like my own journey, life is a network of interconnected pathways; at certain junctions, I found people ready to assist me, and at others, I found opportunities to lend my own aid. We should never expect favors from those we have helped because that was never their assignment. Expectation leads to disappointment. Never expect anything in return from those that you have done favors for if you don't want to be disappointed. Favors are from God to be delivered by the angel assigned to you, not from someone you have helped. At the 2020 Haitian Ladies Network book launch, I met Francesca, who shared the same name as my mother. We connected instantly. Within just three months, I found myself flying to New York City for her event titled "I am Forever Evolving." Not only did she organize this function in my honor, but she also named the event after my guest speaker topic, "Adjust Thy Crown."

I presented my book to a room full of young to middle-aged women. I was on cloud nine.

Balancing Life's "Pearls of Women Network," Pearls of Wisdom, Pearls of Life, House of New Vision and Hope, HANA Miami, and HANA International are just a few of the Haitian Diaspora groups that have extended a hand to me with the launch of my book, and for that I am grateful. The Haitian people of South Florida have welcomed me and have reconnected me to my Haitian roots.

I continued to expand my reach and influence, this time beyond Washington, D.C. and South Florida. I was invited for an in-person keynote presentation at Voorhees College in South Carolina. This event was super special as it was to celebrate Black History Month, and it was at my alma mater. My friends Ann and Sharon orchestrated an impressive book launch at Sandal Beach Resort in Barbados. With around one hundred and fifty attendees, the event was graced by the presence of my son and his family, who flew in specifically for the launch. My friend Sheila came in from Canada, while Guerda and Marie Denise joined me from Florida.

This launch turned into an extended vacation. The event featured drummers, dancers, food, and music for all in attendance to eat, dance and be merry. I signed and sold over fifty copies of *Girls Can Move Mountains* during the course of the event.

In the chilly early months of 2020, shortly after my book had seen the light of day, I found myself cozily tucked into my condo in the heart of Maryland. As the winter sun streamed through the window, the shrill ring of my phone cut through the silence.

It was a call from my dear friend Eric. "I have a young couple here for a few days visiting with me. I want you to meet them. Can I bring them over?"

All I had a chance to ask was, "When?"

Eric answered, "Now."

It was clear that I had no other choice but to say yes, and of course, I did.

They were at my condo unit so quickly that I felt he must have made the call while driving on my street. Before long, I had three adults and a two-year-old in my apartment, and we had the best of times. I had lunch delivered, took all of my grandkid's toys out of the toy chest, and here I was on the floor playing nana with a brand new two-year-old. We took many pictures. I gave Rachel a copy of *Girls Can Move Mountains,* and they left.

Fast forward to March 2021. I once again received a call from my good friend Eric informing me that Rachel wanted to connect with me. He had to refresh my memory as to who Rachel was. "She wanted to invite you," he said, "to present your book to a group of movie directors at the film festival in Cannes, France."

All I could say was, "OMG! Life is full of surprises." I paused for a minute, thinking, "If only I had said no to Eric when he wanted to bring this couple and the two-year-old to my condo...I would never have had the opportunity to meet Rachel. And now I am going to a film festival in France." If only I had gotten upset when I was rejected from sharing the *Washington Women's Magazine* at the Haitian Ladies Network Brunch and stopped attending their function, I would never have had this tremendous international book launch. I firmly believe that life isn't like a box of chocolates, where you never know what you're going to get. Instead, I'm convinced that you reap from life what you sow into it. It pays to be nice, kind, and grateful.

I flew to France and had the best time at the Cannes Film Festival. I found myself rubbing shoulders with acclaimed personalities, engaging in lively dinners, and dancing amidst a whirl of glitz and glamor. At the villa, I met Iris and spontaneously had an international live podcast, in addition to being invited by her to be a speaker at the International World Women's Empowerment Conference in Dubai. Among the many faces at the film festival, I had the pleasure of meeting Kenny, a standout character with his unique charm and wit. Kenny is a black financier who assists his clients in investing in movies. Through Kenny, I met Dr. Bordash, a filmmaker and professor of script writing at New York University, who believes my book has strong potential for a television documentary or even a big-screen movie.

The course my life has taken is truly mind-boggling. An example of this unexpected journey occurred in Dubai, where my book received a Book of the Year award from the Orion Stars Award. I met another group of world-renowned women who care deeply about global women's empowerment and invited me to participate in their functions.

Suddenly, my sphere of influential people in women's empowerment, entertainment, and movies is growing by leaps and bounds. I am at a point of selecting which function to attend because of distance, time zone changes, and the toll these travels can take on one's body. The crystal and beautifully framed awards and proclamations decorate the walls and tables in my home, all because of the visibility I received from the book. I even had a day named after me in Miami Dade by our Haitian sister Council Member Irving who proclaimed November 14, 2021, as Dr. Solanges Vivens Day.

In *Girls Can Move Mountains,* I described a moment in time when I was encouraged by my sister Mirlene to build a school in a province called Meyer in Jacmel, Haiti, a province that I had never visited. The school was built to assist the poor villagers who could not afford to send their children to school due to financial constraints and for those who lived in orphanages. From the early to the mid-2000s, many of the children who attended Centre d'études classiques de Meyer were educated free of charge.

Many of those children are today adult professionals in the medical field as physicians and nurses. Some are pilots, teachers, engineers, and other well-recognized professionals.

Fast forward to 2023, when I received the Nelson Mandela Children's Fund award at the film festival in Nice, France, all because of this endeavor. It was thrilling to have had my sister Mirlene walking the red carpet and on stage with me accepting this once-in-a-lifetime award.

CANNES, FRANCE

My brother Jean Claude came along as our bodyguard and trusted driver. From Nice, we flew to Paris and rented a car.

From Paris, we drove to Sainte Solange to attend the Pentecost Monday pilgrimage.

We then drove cross-country for an entire week visiting churches, basilicas, and massive cathedrals throughout France before returning to Florida.

During my stay at the villa for the Mandela function, an invitation came my way. I was to speak at the Better World Fund's Masterclass Conference for Women Empowerment, scheduled for September during the film festival in Venice, Italy. For each event I attended, I got invited to speak at another big or bigger function.

VENICE, ITALY

As a rule, I support, attend and speak at functions that deal mainly with children's education and women's empowerment. My goal is always to have an enjoyable moment—I meet new people, make new friends and engagements, and hope to have made a difference. As we age, although opportunities to make new friends might appear to lessen, attending social functions breathes fresh air into our lives, keeping us active, relevant, and brimming with joy. As a widow, I've learned that attending functions with the primary objective of finding a partner can often lead to disappointment. Instead, I focus on the experience itself and the people I get to meet. The key is to always be in the present, focus on enjoying the moment, leaving behind a beautiful and lasting impression.

My sharing of those accolades and wisdom is by no means patting myself on the back or showing off. My goal is to play an active role while in retirement, empowering women and showing what is possible. As I write this book, I am seventy-seven years old. I must admit that twenty, thirty, and even fifty years ago, if a numerologist, a palmist, or a voodoo priest had predicted this present period in my life, I would have accused this predictor of being insane.

I am writing this last chapter while on a ten-day cruise in the Galapagos Islands with my twenty-year-old grandson.

When I am asked *why*, I always answer *why not*. I write and speak out to educate, elevate, inspire, motivate, and encourage. My age bears no weight on my behavior, my thought process, or my perception of life.

When I talk to my grandson and other young adults, I ask them to smile and even giggle. It is not as bad as it seems to be. Whatever happened had already taken place; it is behind us. More often than not, there is nothing we can do about it. Accept it as a fact and move on. My advice is to be prepared, take calculated risks, choose who you allow in your theater, and always be vigilant.

At his tender age of sixty-five, I lost my husband and was faced with the daunting challenge of forging ahead on my own. I miss him every day, yet I know he will never return. I dream of him often, and I wake up realizing it was yet another dream, not a reality. I thank him for the visit, and I go along with my day until our love rekindles again in heaven.

Life is lived in the present and is often only understood when we look back on it. For instance, we might not understand why certain things happened in the past until we reach a point where we can see the overall trajectory of our lives. With every breath we take, we create our own narrative, each day adding a new page to the book of our life's journey. And with the last breath, the act is over, the curtain is closed, and the last chapter of life is written.

However, there is a dash between the date we were born and the date we die. The dash is the life that we live today in the present. It is up to us to write our history as we live and never allow anyone nor anything to change the narrative. So I pray that once I die, I will become one of God's traveling angels. My hope is to deliver favors on earth to his charitable, kind, well-behaved, and beloved children.

Turtle Wisdom: Never Forget Your Roots

Just as turtles instinctively traverse vast ocean distances to return to the very beach they were born on, the story of this chapter embodies that enduring pull of our roots, a magnetic force that tugs at the heartstrings. As I carved my niche on foreign American soil, my Haitian heritage remained unforgotten, hibernating like a seed nestled in the earth, waiting for the right conditions to break free. The Haitian Ladies Network was the nurturing rain shower, coaxing that dormant seed into sprouting vibrant shoots. Even as my American story unfolded, graced with success and recognition, a parallel narrative was written in bold, vibrant strokes, one of re-awakening, a renewed sense of identity and purpose, derived from my reconnection with my roots.

As life unfolds, we often traverse pathways far from the shores we originally set sail from, propelled by career aspirations, golden opportunities, or the unpredictable whirlwind of circumstances. The intrinsic need to stay true to one's roots, irrespective of the geographical span or the vast social expanse, is a sentiment that resonates universally. Our roots are the anchoring threads that bind us, molding our identities and deeply etched value systems. They provide a stabilizing foundation, cocooning us, nourishing our growth, and bestowing a rich tapestry of cultural wealth onto our lives. Thus, no matter where we find ourselves on the world map, it becomes vital to find unique, meaningful ways to retain that umbilical connection with our roots. In our multicultural, globalized era, it's a call to honor our individual heritage even as we rejoice in the diverse medley of cultures around us.

TURTLE INSIGHTS

1. Our heritage is not merely an echo from the past; it is an intimate, living part of us, influencing our perspectives and decisions. Reflect on what your cultural roots mean to you. How have they imprinted upon your life and the choices you've made?

2. Have there been moments when you felt your connection with your roots becoming tenuous? Reflect on those instances. What repercussions did that disconnection have on you?

3. Staying connected to your heritage in your present lifestyle can be an enriching endeavor. Reflect on the ways you maintain this connection. Is it through music, food, language, or traditions?

4. Contemplate ways to further solidify your ties with your roots. Could it be through travel, exploring your culture's history, or engaging more deeply with your community? Reflect on how this enhanced connection could catalyze your personal evolution.

5. Think of a time when reconnecting with your roots became a light of hope, helped you surmount an obstacle, or ushered in a positive transformation in your life. What insights did it offer you? As turtles show us, no matter how far we roam, there is profound wisdom in never forgetting our roots.

AFFIRMATIONS

- My roots shape my identity, and I am proud of my heritage.
- I celebrate my cultural heritage and embrace the diversity around me.
- My roots ground me, give me strength, and guide my journey forward.
- I honor my past and use it as a guidepost for my future.
- Like a turtle, I remember my beginnings and carry them with me as I navigate my path.

A Tribute to the Unyielding Spirit

As you've turned the pages of this book, you've journeyed with me through the ups and downs that life has to offer. You've seen me fight through sorrow, battle tough times, and question societal norms. You've accompanied me in the nerve-wracking silence of meeting rooms and across the inspiring breadth of our world. You've felt the sting of discrimination and also savored the cozy warmth of companionship.

I am a woman who's experienced life much like you have. I've loved deeply, hurt greatly, stumbled, learned, and picked myself up again. In telling my story, I've aimed to be completely open and brave, never avoiding my own missteps and imperfections. Because it's in these imperfect moments that we find life's wisdom, making us stronger and more empowered as we grow older.

The experiences I've shared aren't just my own; they're part of the broader human experience. We all come up against hurdles that seem too high to clear. We all face loss, failure, and life's unpredictability. But if there's one lesson to learn from my journey, it's that we all have the power to get up, rebuild, and define ourselves anew.

By sharing my story, my goal has been to highlight the inner strength we each possess—the power to shatter expectations, welcome change, and forge our own path in life. I hope I've shown the importance of not giving up, of being flexible, and of never stopping learning, even when we face huge challenges. The tests we face don't define us; it's how we respond to them that does.

One thing I hope you remember from my journey is the value of resilience—a quality that isn't about brute force, but about being flexible in spirit. It's about being like bamboo in a storm, bending, not breaking. It's about having the courage to stay hopeful and keep going, even when you've been knocked down.

Whether you're an ambitious woman starting your career, a leader steering through the choppy waters of business, or someone older navigating the highs and lows of aging, I hope my story has offered you a ray of hope and a source of motivation.

As I look to what lies ahead, I feel a sense of excitement for the journey yet to come. I may not know what the future holds, but I do know that every new day brings a new adventure, a new lesson, and a new tale to tell.

So, as we wrap up my story, I hope you keep these tales close to your heart. Let them guide you, soothe you, and inspire you. Take the wisdom that speaks to you, and let it light your way. And always remember, we all have the power to do incredible things, so dream big, believe in yourself, and be the hero of your own story.

Here's to living life fearlessly and fully, embracing change, daring to be yourself, making the impossible possible, and most importantly, knowing that the best is yet to come.